FOCUS FORECASTING AND DRP

FOCUS FORECASTING AND DRP

Logistics Tools of the Twenty-first Century

Bernard T. Smith

VANTAGE PRESS
New York

To my children, their children, and to the
skinny people in the wards

Contents

FOCUS FORECASTING AND DRP

Chapter One

Purpose of This Book

Sometimes the kids want to know where you're coming from. My son Christopher is the president of B. T. Smith and Associates. I work for him as a consultant. We market forecasting and inventory management software primarily in the microcomputer network area, but also for mainframes and minicomputers.

There were a lot of mixed feelings writing this book. My first inclination was to write it with Steve Johnston because of the programming work he'd done making some of my early forecasting concepts available to many different companies around the world. Steve didn't really have the time to write a book with me, and when I finished writing it on my own he wasn't sure he agreed with what I wrote.

My first choice for publishing the book was Oliver Wight Associates because of my longtime friendship with Ollie himself and with the Oliver Wight organization. But here again I found many conflicts with what I believe to be practical concepts of inventory management versus some of the concepts the Oliver Wight people teach as gospel.

Perhaps it was almost dying from cancer of the pancreas in 1987 and my so valuing the remaining days left to me now that made me choose to write this book and brave the wrath of some of my peers. Its purpose is to present to you clearly and sometimes abrasively what I've learned in fourteen years as an MIS (Management Information Systems) person and fourteen years as a vice president of inventory control and from my consulting visits to over 150 companies in different parts of the world, where I must admit I learned more than I taught.

Write it down when you disagree with me. I treasure abrasive dissent. It scrapes away to get at the kernel of truth. One of my clients taught me that. Sorry I don't remember which one.

May you find this book something of value.

1

PART I

Chapter Two

Objectives of Inventory Management

My boss, Attila, made me vice president of inventory control on the day he was made president of the company.

Attila said, "Smith, this company is a cooperative. That means our board of directors are our customers. The one quick way that I, Attila, can get fired is to run out of stock. You, Smith, are my new inventory control vice president. If we run out of stock and I get fired you can bet that I will have accepted your resignation one month earlier. Have you got that?" He put his hands on my shoulders and made sure he had my attention.

All year I worked hard reviewing inventory, expediting, increasing safety stock, developing alternate suppliers, establishing U.S. backups for my import programs, walking around the warehouses checking empty shelves that hadn't been restocked from reserves, slapping the wrists of order fillers who didn't climb ladders to fill orders from backup stock, chasing people around Receiving to put away goods. We had by year end the highest service level in the history of the company. I expected an "atta boy," a raise, and a promotion to senior vice president.

Attila said, "Smith, you're running the company right down a rat hole! Have you been out in the warehouse lately? Of course not. They'd kill you on sight out there. There's no room to turn around out there. And if our finance VP catches you, you're dead meat. The bank is going to drop our credit rating. Can you believe a company as big as ours brought to its knees by your stupid inventory excesses?"

Attila grasped my shoulders again. "Smith, get rid of those excesses and don't create any more. But don't forget, stay in stock on the things we need. Have you got that?'' He shook me by the shoulders to make his point.

What could I do? I ran a 30 percent off excess discount bulletin right away. I'm a simple person. That seemed the best approach. Our customers and employees loved it. My wife still has a 30 percent off Panasonic TV we personally bought from the discount bulletin. It was wonderful the inventory was going down, the service level was going up, the sales were going up. What could be better?

What else could I do? I told the buyers: No more big buys. Buy what we need. Forget the big-buy discounts. No more container-load or truckload buys cluttering up the warehouse. The operations people loved me. At the end of the year we still had the highest service in the history of the company and the inventory turnover was great, too! Here comes my ''atta boy,'' a raise, maybe even executive vice president.

Attila said, ''Smith, you're out of your mind. One more year like this and we're out of business. Our gross profit is the pits. It's barely over our operating costs. We've got more loss-leaders than KMart. No more dumping. No discount bulletins. Get your act together or get out. Have you got that?'' This time he did not put his hands on my shoulders. He acted like he was afraid of catching something.

What could I do? I had to keep up service. I had to keep up the turnover. I could not let the gross profit go down. Then it struck me. Quick Response, Just In Time, Kanban, more frequent review. Eureka! We had been reviewing once a month and twice a month. I started reviewing twice a week and once a week. I started buying our best sellers every time they ran low. Talk about turns; the inventory never even warmed up. It came in the warehouse in one door and went out the other. Every time Receiving turned around in came another shipment ready to be restocked.

Of course with so many inbound shipments Receiving got backed up. So I made up a computer system that measured how much customer service we lost because of goods backed up on our receiving dock. From then on whenever the service level went down I'd tell Attila how much service level was piled up on the dock and he would twist the operations VP's head around until the warehouse fixed the problem. Of course the operations VP worked his crews a lot of overtime and had to hire some housewives and students to help out.

Boy, by the end of the year . . . high customer service . . . high inventory turnover . . . good gross profit. For sure at least an "atta boy."

Attila said, "Bernie, you had a good year." He almost had a tear in his eye as he gave me a raise. Then he said, "I wish you would go talk to our operations VP. He's running the company right down a rat hole. His cost of operation is out of sight. He can't seem to get his people to do the job without overtime. I'm afraid he's losing it."

When I visited the operations VP he just barely resisted grabbing me by the throat and choking me to death. It took Attila five years to figure out what was happening.

No person here is a real person. This is just a fictitious example of what can happen if a company doesn't measure all four of the fundamental objectives of inventory management.

For sound inventory management measure the right things and measure all four them . . . every month and versus last year:

Service   # of out of stock or
           line fill rate or
           dollar fill rate or
           delivered when requested

Turns   Next 12 periods forecast
           divided by average inventory

Gross   The aggregate gross profit
           this year versus last year

Work   The lines of receiving or
           the number of production starts and
           the freight in and out

These measures can be traded one for the other like a kernel on an ear of corn. Measure only one and the others will get worse. Measure all four and your business will prosper.

The next chapter is about logistics. Logistics is a part of the science of inventory management that has a favorable impact on all four of these basic objectives.

Chapter Three

Logistics

It's the right stuff in the right place at the right time.

Higher-quality and lower-cost distribution of goods and services is a new frontier. It's called logistics. Its goals are:

Better customer service
Higher inventory turnover
Higher gross profit
Reduced work
Higher-quality business life

Logistics managers use new tools to make these things happen. They use computer forecasting instead of guessing. They use scheduling instead of reorder points. They study and use the latest forecasting and scheduling tools: Focus Forecasting and DRP (Distribution Resource Planning). They measure results.

These people are perfectly positioned. Inventories are imbalanced, thus hiding company profit weaknesses. Companies have taken for granted low transportation costs and have shortsightedly closed major distribution facilities. Return on investment measures of performance have all but been forgotten in the push for higher earnings per share and higher income-statement bottom lines. Customer service and marketing objectives have overwhelmed good business sense.

These forces are pushing the need for logistics managers and systems at a frantic pace. Just look at the National Association of Physical Distribution Management changing its name to the Council of Logistics Management. In the want ads the title "Vice President Logistics" is replacing titles like Vice President Administration, Vice

President Distribution, and Vice President Operations. Companies hope these logistics managers and their new systems can correct inventories that are imbalanced with both excesses and out-of-stocks.

Inventory Excesses

In factories right now people are using expensive machinery to produce goods that will sit in warehouses for years. Meanwhile customers are trying to get goods that those same factories are too busy to produce.

Management is sitting on inventory excess. To dispose of the excess inventory quickly would devastate company profits.

Inventory can hide company weakness. There is strong incentive for a company with declining sales to continue to overproduce. The production absorbs the company overhead and puts it in an asset called inventory. Companies have at this moment inventories of products that will sit on their shelves for years and finally be crushed in compactors. There is strong incentive for companies not to dispose of these excesses. Disposal programs devalue the excess inventory. In some companies these devaluations can offset the entire year's profit. Most company presidents choose rather to carry the excess; after all, interest costs are relatively low. These decisions put terrible burdens on the near-term future of the company. The day of reckoning comes when interest rates rise.

Oil prices are still relatively low. Transportation costs since deregulation of common carriers have been low. Customer service pressures are enormous and outweigh reasonable distribution decisions. Companies just looking at the short term have been closing large distribution centers and opening smaller ones at customer sites. Multiple distribution centers with duplicate inventories and duplicate supervisory staffs are expensive. The day of reckoning comes as fuel costs rise.

Traditional company measurement systems stress gross margin, sales growth, earnings per share, and cost control. Unfortunately, for periods of time all of these can be purchased by sacrificing return on investment, especially inventory investment. Some companies at this moment do not even measure return on investment. Vendors offer deals to customers who buy full packs or truckload quantities. Deals

9

mean higher gross profit for buying container loads, freight cars, and truckloads, but rarely do these deals mean higher return on investment for the buyer. The lower return on investment penalty is hidden in the inventory buildup on the balance sheet. Companies falsely believe higher gross profit margins will continue. The day of reckoning comes when capital is no longer available for the next deal.

Look at your company. Walk through the warehouses. See last year's inventory tags. Look at the dust that makes the cartons look like part of the fixtures. And the sad thing is that with all of these excesses, out-of-stocks are just as common in the same companies that have the excesses.

Out-of-stocks

We can't get enough of the right stuff to our customer.

Purolator, Federal Express, Delta Dash, Emery Air Freight, and others have become giants almost overnight. This is part of a feeble attempt to make up for out-of-stocks and goods and services in the wrong place.

Books urge us to do the unreasonable to meet customer expectations, and we do. Company customer service departments answering questions on poor delivery are larger than some departments responsible for delivering the goods on time in the first place. This is another part of the feeble attempt to make up for goods and services in the wrong place.

Companies have elaborate backup warehouse schemes that waste thousands of dollars in extra freight making up for goods in the wrong place. They spend five- and six-figure sums on elaborate allocation systems because they can't get enough of the right goods manufactured in the first place. Some companies have gone so far as to buy goods from their competitors to fill customer orders.

Logistics is the process of getting the right goods to the right place in the first place. Logistics avoids inventory excesses and out-of-stocks in the first place by using improved scheduling techniques like DRP.

Improved Forecasting

In the past five years there have been tremendous advances made in the field of forecasting. This has occurred primarily because of the increase in the storage capacity and speed of relatively low-cost microcomputers.

In the past, one of the most popular forms of business forecasting was a statistical approach called exponential smoothing. It used an approximation of a moving average in order to save on the limited computer storage and lack of computer speed at the time. Exponential smoothing systems generally combine these approximations of moving averages with trends and seasonality to create forecasts of the future. This statistical forecasting technique has been around since shortly after World War II, when computers were slow and had limited storage.

In 1978 an entirely new concept of forecasting based on the computer's ability to simulate, called Focus Forecasting, has been added to the world of logistics. Since November of 1984 over four hundred companies have switched their forecasting to this concept.

Focus Forecasting has three main features not usually part of traditional forecasting approaches:

1. Simplicity
2. Lack of file maintenance
3. The user understands how it works

Simplicity

Most companies that do not have formalized forecasting systems rely on simplistic rules of thumb to forecast future sales of their products. They use things like "we'll probably sell what we sold last year" or "we'll sell what we sold in the last three months." Unlike statistical approaches, Focus Forecasting does not replace these simple techniques with esoteric approaches like exponential smoothing, econometric modeling, cumulative line ratio projections, or least squares regression analysis. Rather, Focus Forecasting uses the simple rule-of-thumb techniques that the company has used for years. It just

11

harnesses the computer's speed to try out these techniques on the product's past history to see which one works the best.

Every time Focus Forecasting forecasts a product it tries out all of the rules of thumb on the product's past history to find the one best rule of thumb for the product at this moment in time.

Lack of File Maintenance

Most statistical forecasting techniques require a great deal of manual coding. People must tell the statistical approach that this is a seasonal product or that this is a basic product. They usually have to code whether an item is high-volume or sporadic. They even have to tell the statistical system whether the item is new or not. People have to tell these systems what curves to expect in the future.

Focus Forecasting does not require as much file maintenance because the forecasting system itself is constantly focusing on the product's particular characteristics. It's continually switching to the technique that is best forecasting this product's historic behavior at this time.

The User Understands How It Works

Since Focus Forecasting uses the very techniques the company has always used, the people who use the forecasts understand how they work already.

For example, Focus Forecasting may tell the user that it picked the formula that "we'll probably sell what we sold last year." There is no need to explain things like alpha factors or seasonality curves, how to calculate square roots, or why sines and cosines describe trends and product sales patterns. The user can either accept that the company will probably sell what it sold last year or disagree. The understanding is already there.

One company with Focus Forecasting is projecting sales for over 165,000 products by location. The people who use the Focus Forecasting output change less than 8 percent of the system's decisions.

Logistics managers use Focus Forecasting as the mechanical part of their gross requirements to drive their scheduling systems. These more accurate forecasts require fewer move-up and delay decisions. Focus Forecasting is an ideal front end to improved scheduling.

Improved Scheduling

DRP Distribution Resource Planning is an improved scheduling system. It is a major improvement over reorder point systems. Reorder point systems launch new orders for inventory replenishment. They generally involve decisions to order or not to order and to expedite or not to expedite. Companies used reorder points to deploy inventory even before the first computers.

DRP is a scheduling system that has major advantages over reorder point systems:

1. DRP not only orders and expedites, but unorders and delays as well. When actual demand meets or exceeds forecast, both reorder point systems and DRP order more and expedite open orders. When actual demand falls short of forecast, however, only DRP cancels open orders and delays future orders. Reorder point systems simply don't order any more.
2. DRP tells suppliers what orders to expect in the future. Reorder point systems surprise suppliers with random orders as goods are needed. DRP projects planned orders far into the future so that suppliers can secure raw materials and production capacity. The supplier can be an outside vendor or the company's own factory. In either case, suppliers do a better job of providing goods and services when they have projections of their customer's future needs.
3. DRP is not just an inventory replenishment system, but a way of scheduling resources for the whole business. Gross requirements, scheduled receipts, projected on-hand, and planned orders can be extended in value, weight, cube, worker hours, and machine hours. These projections allow companies to look at the lack of capacity or underutilization of warehouse space, trucking, cash, and labor before they become a reality.
4. DRP provides action messages telling the logistics person when things go wrong and what action needs to be taken. These messages get at the root of the inventory management problems. If

13

the forecasts are too low, the warehouse loses inventory, or the supplier doesn't ship promptly, DRP shows how the problem occurred and prepares to correct the shortfall. If the forecasts are too high, a customer returns a large shipment, or a vendor ships a special buy early, again DRP shows the cause of the problem and prepares to take corrective action.

5. DRP supplies joint inventory replenishment logic. It fills truck-loads, carloads, and container-loads with a mix of products balancing the weeks of supply across the product line. It allocates how arriving containers should break bulk to various distribution centers or stores. When vendors come in with "such a deal," DRP calculates the increase in inventory investment to meet the deal minimum and tells the logistics person how many weeks' supply will result from the decision.

Logistics managers use DRP to reschedule resources within and outside the company as real-world situations change from day to day. Focus Forecasting makes the best possible statement of what the future will be, but if, as with all forecasts, it is wrong, DRP reschedules as the actual supply and demand for goods and services develop and as Focus Forecasting reforecasts what the future will be based on the latest real-world data.

The next chapter looks in more detail at the Focus Forecasting concept and logic.

PART II

Chapter Four

Focus Forecasting—the Concept

People in companies use simple rules to forecast the future sales of goods and services all the time. They use rules like:

1. We'll probably sell what we sold last year.
2. We'll probably sell 10 percent more than last year.
3. We'll probably sell what we sold the last quarter.
4. We'll probably sell half as much as we did in the last six months.

Focus Forecasting can take these simple rules and try them out on an item to see how they worked in the past. Generally some rules work better for some items than for others. Generally some rules work better at certain times of the year. Every time Focus Forecasting makes a forecast for an item, it tries all the rules on the past sales for this item to pick the one rule that would have worked best to forecast this item's past sales. That rule should be the best choice to forecast the future sales of this item now.

An Example of Focus Forecasting

Over the years we've played "Can You Outguess Focus Forecasting?" with thousands of people. One of the examples we use is based on sales of five-tined manure forks out of a warehouse in eastern Pennsylvania. The sales history for the past eighteen months looks like this: (see page 18)

The name of the game is to guess how many five-tine manure forks will be sold out of the warehouse in total for the next three

Month	Last Year	This Year
1	18	2
2	12	18
3	10	21
4	3	4
5	8	9
6	6	2
7	16	**
8	18	**
9	29	**
10	12	
11	15	
12	13	

months. It's a one-number answer. A total for all three months. Your guess is _____?

Make sure you guess before you turn to the answer. Forecasting is always easy when you know what actually happened. . . .

Focus Forecasting guessed sixty-three. Focus Forecasting guessed that we will sell as many five-tine manure forks in the next three months as we did last year in the next three months.

Focus Forecasting made believe it was only month 3 of this year. It forecast months 4 through 6 of this year using all four of the simple rules:

	1	2	3	4	5	6	7	8	9	10	11	12
Last Year	18	12	10	3	8	6	16	18	29	12	15	13
This Year	2	18	21	4	9	2	**	**	**			

A. We'll probably sell what we sold last year. 17

B. We'll probably sell 10 percent more than last year 18.7

C. We'll probably sell what we sold the last quarter. 41

D. We'll probably sell half as much as we did in the last six months. 40.5

The actual number of sales 4 through 6 of this year was fifteen. So Focus Forecasting picked rule A to forecast months 7 through 9. Last year's sales in 7 through 9 were sixty-three.

Going back one quarter to select a rule is called an iteration. Different companies find that different numbers of iterations do the best job of picking accurate rules for an item. To forecast sales of five-tine manure forks in this example, Focus Forecasting went back one iteration to pick one of the four rules to forecast future sales. Companies use one to twelve iterations to find the best rules to fit their items.

As months go by, Focus Forecasting will adjust to the sales pattern an item is showing. It will switch to rules that do a better job of forecasting an item's sales behavior. For this reason there is little manual intervention needed in working with a Focus Forecasting system.

The Focus Forecasting concept is as follows:

1. Use simple rules.
2. Test the rules to find out which one worked best for this item.
3. Use that rule to forecast the future sales.

Companies use Focus Forecasting for financial planning, for marketing projections, and as the first step in inventory management.

Focus Forecasting can forecast sales for all of the items in a company that have a sales history. If no one in the company knows something the sales history does not show, Focus Forecasting can outguess any person in the company. It uses simple rules. People understand how it works. People should not override the mechanical forecasts unless they know something the system does not know. It's a reliable way to begin inventory management.

The next chapter tells about the history of Focus Forecasting so far.

Chapter Five

Focus Forecasting History

Where Focus Forecasting Came From . . . The Concept

Back in the 1960s the first computers became available at a price that businesses other than the government could afford. A great number of very complicated solutions to simple problems sprang up. It was the age of operations research: linear programming, the Simplex method, the Northwest Corner procedure, Boolean algebra, adding, subtracting, and multiplying with ones, inclusive ands and ors, normal distributions and Poisson distributions, and even Walodi Weibull's Statistics of Extremes. The Ph.D.'s and the college professors were running rampant trying mathematical approaches to solving relatively simple business problems. These solutions rarely worked.

I remember working with Jeremiah Cantor from the Honeywell Industry Research Council. Together we set up a retail inventory replenishment system based on E. J. Gumbull's interpretation of Weibull's Statistics of Extremes. We reasoned that since Statistics of Extremes dealt with forecasting rare events like floods and tornadoes, it should be well suited to forecasting retail sales, since they were also rare events. Perhaps Jerry understood it; I certainly didn't. The most we could print was one item on a page. We were experimenting with Shillitos in Cincinnati. They had five stores with eight hundred stock-keeping units in each store. The buyer gave it her best try, but she was never able to get it off the ground. I can still remember Jerry and me in the back room counting the products, shaking the boxes, and shaking our heads.

Not long after, Jack Sparrow from J. C. Penney taught me the semiautomatic stock control procedure for retail inventory replenishment. Basically, it went along these lines: if you sell one, buy one.

In appendix 1 of my previous book, *Focus Forecasting: Computer Techniques for Inventory Control* (Essex Junction, VT: Oliver Wight Limited Publications, 1984), you can find the details of J. C. Penney's replace sales system. For now it's sufficient to say it was a very simple approach and it worked like magic. It costs less than a penny an item sold to replenish retail inventories. As the director of information systems for Warnaco Corporation, I had over 180 department stores across the United States on that system.

There was a saying in the sixties: KISS (Keep It Simple, Stupid). The KISS concept is one of the main foundations of Focus Forecasting.

In those days I had the chance to work with some great people, people like Dave Zaversky, the father of IBM's Retail Impact; people like Bob Brown, the man who applied exponential smoothing in hundreds, maybe thousands of companies in different parts of the world; people like Phil Brail from the Litton Corporation, who did more for vendor common source marking than any man I knew. But the man who had the most impact on me was Oliver Wight.

Ollie worked in Bridgeport, Connecticut, at the same time I did. Those were the days when companies were just starting to use MRP (Material Requirements Planning). If Ollie taught me any one thing, it was "if it works, keep doing it." Ollie was always interested in learning anything new about systems and inventory management. One day he came over to see me at Warner's World Famous Girdles and Bras on Layette Street in Bridgeport. At the local APICS meeting in Fairfield he had heard about something I was doing that was a new twist on MRP.

My buyers didn't trust MRP. They were using exponential smoothing to forecast raw material usage. The MRP showed dramatic changes in future raw material requirements based on upcoming production when the buyers compared it to the exponential smoothing forecasts based on prior usage. So in order to prove to the buyers and to myself that the MRP was accurate, we started to use Computer Output Microfilm (COM). We had the computer records sent to a microfilm processing company, and they ran all of the detail transactions from one raw material balance to the next raw material balance. If the buyers ever questioned any of the MRP balances, they could use the computer output microfilm to verify all the transactions leading up to the new balance. I showed it to Ollie, and I was a little embarrassed because by then MRP was considered state-of-the-art.

I was embarrassed that my buyers didn't trust MRP and that I had to prove to them that the balances were right. Ollie said simply, "Don't be silly, Bernie; if it works, do it." To me that was the second part of the foundation for Focus Forecasting. If it works, do it.

An inventory management consultant from Booz Allen interviewed me for an inventory management position at American Hardware. The consultant asked me, "What system will you use for American Hardware?" And I said, "Well, we'll probably use whatever works," and he kept coaching me trying to force me to say that we'd use the exponential smoothing, trend, cycle, seasonality, noise, philosophy of the time. But relentlessly I said, "We'll do what works." Of course at the time I didn't know of anything else that worked or even anything else that didn't work.

Coopers and Lybrand's Dr. Shegda had installed exponential smoothing in American Hardware Supply. At that time American Hardware had three distribution centers, with about thirty thousand items in each center. They had one warehouse on the exponential smoothing system Dr. Shegda had installed. At the other two warehouses they just took last year's sales times a factor to project what their future requirements would be. Neither system worked very well. The buyers changed half of the computer's decisions.

There was one other phenomenon that was happening in the late sixties. The operations research people and college professors had been trying to use complicated solutions to business problems and had some spectacular failures. The people who actually ran the businesses—the inventory managers, plant managers, manufacturing vice presidents—laid out their failures royally in article after article.

So the professors, consultants, and systems people at the time had a brilliant idea. It was called involve the user. The idea was that if you involved the user right from the start, he couldn't so readily point the finger at your failure. So another ingredient in Focus Forecasting was involving the user.

All twenty-one of American Hardware's buyers were changing the computer's decisions of how much to buy. These buyers would be involved in the creation of Focus Forecasting. They were well suited, since they were using little systems of their own just to change the computer's buy. The oldest buyer was a man from New England whose name was Howard Clark, the lawn and garden buyer. He said, "Forecasting isn't all that difficult. All you have to do is look at last year and look at this year and whatever percentage you're running ahead of last year, just figure it's going to keep on going." Well, that involved the user but sounded a little too simple.

There was another user, a young fellow named Norman Riffner; he was the plumbing buyer. He also felt that forecasting really wasn't that difficult. "All you have to do is whatever you sold the last three months, just figure you'll sell that the next three months." Again that sounded a little too simple.

There were twenty-one buyers and each one of them had his own little formula for forecasting the future. I hadn't yet given up on the old standby exponential smoothing. And there were still some of the latest esoterics, like Cogs or react or cumulative line ratio and others too obscure to include in those mentioned here. I tried out the different techniques on different sets of data and some techniques worked well for some data and some techniques worked well on other data—which is fine for involving a lot of people, but made creating a computer system next to impossible.

So here were the three ingredients to create Focus Forecasting:

1. Keep it simple.
2. If it works, keep doing it.
3. Involve the users.

John Berryman, the president of American Hardware, hired me as inventory supervisor. He just recently passed away, but he probably wouldn't mind my recounting that he was a legend in his own time. He told me himself that he was a legend in his own time. To me he was. There wasn't a topic that John couldn't dominate a conversation on. The last three people who had the inventory management job at American Hardware before me had only lasted two years each. So John Berryman was on top of my list in involving the user. I figured if I did use anything of what he told me I'd at least survive out my two years. I can still remember the day I knocked on his door and opened it and he was lying on the couch taking his morning nap. He sat up, pushed his glasses up his nose, chomped on a fresh cigar, and said, "Yes-s-s-s-s-s-s." I told him that we were trying to create a new forecasting approach for American Hardware and wanted his input.

The words he said to me next are the cornerstone of Focus Forecasting. He said, "Forecasting is relatively simple. The recent past is the best indicator of the future." With that he would have returned to his nap if I didn't press him for more detail. He said, "If it's raining, forecast it's going to rain. If the stock market's going up, forecast the stock market's going to go up."

I left his office and thought about that. It wasn't as stupid as it sounded at first. If you look at any of those charts on the front pages of the *Wall Street Journal* you will see that if personal income is going up, it continues to go up a lot more than it changes directions. As a matter of fact, I could forecast personal income for the past seven years without looking at the *Wall Street Journal*—so could you, incidentally; it's almost a straight line.

The recent past—the best indicator of the future. This concept and some of the simple forecasting techniques the buyers were using and a knowledge of computers created the concept Focus Forecasting. Whatever simple buyer strategy worked the best for forecasting an item in the recent past, that became the strategy for forecasting the future. If Norm Riffner's approach—"whatever you sold the last three months, just figure you'll sell the next three months"—worked the best for this item in forecasting what had already happened in the past three months, that's the strategy picked up for forecasting the next three months. Howard Clark's strategy is "whatever percentage we were running ahead of last year is the percentage ahead of last year we will continue to run." If that worked in the recent past, that's the strategy the computer uses to forecast the future.

And so Focus Forecasting was born. It used simple strategies, the buyers' own little techniques they had been using for years. It involved the user. When Focus Forecasting did its projections it indicated when it was using Howard's approach or Norman's approach. And best of all, Focus Forecasting worked. We installed Focus Forecasting in December of 1972, and it's still running unchanged since that day some seventeen years later.

Focus Forecasting . . . the Software

I remember sitting on Ollie Wight's porch in Newbury, New Hampshire, with his wife, Joan. We were sipping scotch and looking out over Lake Sunapee. Ollie had encouraged me to write the first book on Focus Forecasting. We had great reams of paper with not too much content.

Ollie said, "We've known each other a long time, haven't we?" and I agreed. He said, "You trust me, don't you?"

I said, "Implicitly."

He said, "You've not told anyone American Hardware's seven Focus Forecasting strategies."

I said, "That's right, Ollie."

He said, "But you'll tell me, won't you?" and I kind of shuffled my feet and I said, "I'll tell you, Ollie," and I did. I ran through the seven strategies one by one, perhaps betraying American Hardware's trust, but here he was, Oliver Wight himself, the great man. If you couldn't trust him, whom could you trust?

He looked to Joan and he said, "Did you get that, Joan?"

Joan even in those days had an ample bosom, and she reached down in her bra and pulled out a tape recorder. She rewound it and played it, and it said, "Specki spa ish qrt sqt ish qrt ppt."

It hadn't recorded, for whatever reason, and that was the last time that I ever told anybody American Hardware's specific seven strategies.

Our company questioned what strategy should be added to those that American Hardware already had or, for that matter, what strategies should be removed. So I started to play a game: "Can You Outguess Focus Forecasting?" In the beginning it was innocent enough. I used to take computer printouts of prior demand histories, cover them up with a postcard, and invite people to try to outguess the forecasting system. If they did outguess the forecasting system, I'd take their strategy and incorporate it into the Focus Forecasting model to see whether or not it improved overall accuracy. I never realized how much people enjoyed this game. I have played this game with audiences as large as six hundred people. I have played it with thousands of people in different parts of the world.

At an APICS conference in Las Vegas in Circus Circus in one of the amphitheaters I played "Can You Outguess Focus Forecasting?" with a rather large group. After the meeting, a young man came up to me and asked whether I would go across the street to the MGM Grand to see someone who had written a forecasting software that he wanted to market. Steve Johnston had worked as a contract programmer on an assignment at Carter Carburetor in St. Louis. He had programmed a forecasting model I had consulted with Carter to create. There in a room on the fourth floor Steve demonstrated to me a product called Fortel at that time. I took one look at the demo that he had set up and complained bitterly, "Steve, that's not real data. It's not real data because it's too symmetrical. It displays trend, seasonality, noise, cycles, all the things I know don't exist."

With that I left in a huff. Steve was very persistent. He asked me what he had to do to prove that his system actually did work. So I selected seventy-five items at random from American Hardware's demand history, forecast them with American's existing seven strategies, and measured the accuracy. I gave Steve the same data and challenged him to come up with a system that forecast those seventy-five items as accurately as American Hardware's system. I figured it was a no-lose situation for me. If Steve couldn't outforecast American's seven existing strategies, then he wouldn't pester me anymore about my endorsement of his product. If Steve did outforecast American's seven strategies, well then Steve would be giving American Hardware better forecasting accuracy.

After a lot of hard work Steve's forecasting software did actually outperform the tailor-made programs written internally by American Hardware personnel.

On November 29, 1984, Thanksgiving Day, Steve and I signed an agreement whereby I endorsed his Focus Forecasting software and gave him the exclusive right to market under that product name. For about six years Steve marketed under the Focus Forecasting name and paid me a 20 percent royalty on the software sales. I didn't agree with everything Steve was doing, such as adding in exponential smoothing as part of the formula selection, but I stayed out of his way and let him do his thing. On February 13, 1991, at 10:35 A.M., Steve announced to the International Association of Focus Forecasters that he was changing the name of his company. Shortly after he told me he would no longer be paying me royalties.

Now Christopher markets Focus Forecasting software as part of B. T. Smith and Associates paperless inventory management. We were able to incorporate most of the concepts you find in this book.

We still get people who want to develop their own forecasting software no matter what the cost, no matter what the risk of sacrificing accuracy. It's a fun thing to do with a computer. Well, three thoughts:

1. Focus Forecasting is copyrighted and is a registered trademark, so don't call it Focus Forecasting.
2. At least make sure you read and understand this book.
3. If you do come up with a Focus Forecasting concept or formula more accurate than what Christopher and I are doing, give us a call.

Focus Forecasting was born of necessity in a billion-dollar wholesale company with 165,000 stock-keeping units. It's been running unchanged since December of 1972. The software in one form or another has been available since November of 1984.

In the next chapter are some Focus Forecasting formulas and how to pick the best ones for your company.

Chapter Six

Focus Forecasting Formulas

When you hear the word "formula" it brings to mind integral signs and square roots. That's not what Focus Forecasting formulas are about. If the planner or buyer tells you that one of his or her formulas is "we'll probably sell whatever we sold in the last three months," the Focus Forecasting formula would say $F = Q1$, where $Q1$ is the last three months. Not much of a formula, but when hooked up to the Focus Forecasting evaluation technique when it's selected it can be devastatingly accurate.

How about the buyer or planner who says that we'll probably sell whatever we sold last year? The Focus Forecasting equivalent would be $F = Q4$. In other words, the forecast will be equal to the next three months last year.

So Focus Forecasting formulas are just arithmetic expressions of the everyday rules people use to forecast. Picture a twenty-four-month history. $Q1$ would be the most recent past quarter; $Q2$ would be the quarter before that. The oldest quarter in the twenty-four-month history would be $Q8$.

Buyers and planners can formulate all kinds of nifty forecast formulas expressed in just those simple terms. Of course, there are those of us who must include the rules of a more esoteric nature, such as least squares regression or logarithmic smoothing or sine and cosine wave approximations.

For those formulas something more profound than $Q1$ through $Q8$ is required to express the convolutions of the forecasting system, and that's as it should be . . . no sympathy. The simpler the formula, the more people will believe it and understand it. Never be embarrassed by having too few formulas or too unsophisticated a formula.

American Hardware had seven simple formulas that forecast thirty-three thousand things in five different warehouses. In academic

29

Month	Last Year	This Year	This Year
1	18	2	
2	12	18	
3	10	21	Q4 = 41
4	3	4	
5	8	9	
6	6	2	Q3 = 15
7	16	20	
8	18	24	
9	29	32	Q2 = 76
10	12	18	
11	15	21	
12	13	9	Q1 = 48

research work that I did outside of the company I found in sample data that there actually were four formulas that outperformed those seven formulas. Since forecasting was not an issue at American Hardware, I never pursued replacing the seven formulas with those four formulas and measuring the impact on the total universe. It is possible to improve overall forecast accuracy by removing formulas as well as by adding formulas. Generally speaking, formulas should follow the reasoning and techniques that your inventory management has used effectively in the past.

Sample Formulas

Many times over the years people asked, "We've tried the four formulas shown in *Focus Forecasting: Computer Techniques for Inventory Control.* Could you give us some additional formulas?" In B. T. Smith's Focus Forecasting software there are fifteen different Focus Forecasting formulas. All of the following formulas are in this software. Over the years some of the ones that we've found to be the most effective are:

1. We will probably have the average company increase on this item.

   Let F = the forecast of the future.
   Let Q4 = the demand for the next 3 months last year.
   Let B = the company's expected growth factor.
   Let * = multiplied by.

   So the forecast formula is F = Q4*B.

This is a particularly good rule for highly seasonal items. Take Christmas trees or flyswatters or snow shovels or hoses. Before the season begins, the random increases or decreases in demand preceding this season are not really relevant. Suppose, with Christmas tree bulbs, that during the summertime more people strung up bulbs around their pools so that during the summer there was an increase in the sale of Christmas tree bulbs. That has absolutely nothing to do with the sales of Christmas tree bulbs at Christmas time.

If during harvest season people are using snow shovels to move grain and there is an increase in autumn snow shovel sales over last year, that has nothing to do with the percentage increase or decrease to expect in snow shovel sales during the winter months.

It's a wise formula to be bullish going into season. When the company is out of stock as the season starts, it's very difficult to play catch-up. Generally speaking, out-of-stock in the beginning of the season means playing catch-up throughout the season. Worse yet, delivery of the goods usually finally occurs at the end of the season and the company gets stuck with a carryover for the next season. Please notice what happens here.

The company gets stuck with a carryover for the next season. So the next season, because of the carryover, some companies decide to go lighter at the beginning of the following season. Of course, the same phenomenon happens again. They play catch-up in season, wind up getting the goods when the season is over, and decide to order lighter in advance of the next incoming season. This is called the shoot-yourself-in-the-foot cycle. Companies practicing it long enough and thoroughly enough generally go out of business. Using the average company increase as a formula is probably the best estimate of highly seasonal item sales prior to the beginning of a season. Any worthy attempt at a Focus Forecasting system would include this rule.

2. We'll probably sell what we sold last year.

Let F = the forecast.
Let Q4 = the demand for the next 3 months last year.

So the forecast is $F = Q4$.

This is an excellent rule for highly seasonal items going out of season. Just because we had a tremendous increase in snow shovel sales during the winter season does not mean that we will have an increase in snow shovel sales for the beginning of the following spring. As a matter of fact, if we do have an increase during that period of time, those are only our customers practicing the shoot-yourself-in-the-foot cycle from procedure number 1. Those customers will probably try to return the goods once the early spring is over.

By using "we'll probably sell what we sold last year" we don't purposely run out of inventory. We do try to cover end-of-season sales. People who own swimming pools understand how important this is when they try to get one last thirty-five-pound drum of chlorine tablets in the middle of September. They watch their beautiful pool turn shades of green and yellow. They go from one store to the next, and all they have is five-pound tablets at thirty dollars a tablet. The pool owners grow to hate their retail suppliers. They feel there is a conspiracy against them forcing them to buy thirty-dollar five-pound tablets. Finally they locate one retailer who has the stock of thirty-five-pound tablets at a reasonable price. They become his friend for life. This is why the formula "we'll probably sell what we sold last year" is a viable forecasting approach for end-of-season inventory planning. It doesn't bring us into chasing end-of-season items that will be left over until the following season. But by the same token it does allow us to take prudent risks to remain in stock for our customer. As simpleminded as it sounds, "we'll probably sell what we sold last year" is an excellent rule for our Focus Forecasting family of formulas.

3. We'll probably sell what we sold in the last 3 months.

Let F = the forecast.
Let $Q1$ = the most recent past 3 months.

The formula is $F = Q1$.

This is such a mundane rule that people who have taken APICS certification in more exotic forecasting would normally skip over it. But it is tremendously effective. What can be more an indicator of the recent past than what the demand was the last three months? This stalwart little formula probably is number one in forecasting nonseasonal items. It doesn't overreact because it averages out based on what we sold in the last three months. It doesn't underreact, it's not a six-month or a twelve-month moving average. Because of the way Focus Forecasting is set up, Focus Forecasting won't choose it on seasonal items. On a seasonal item this forecasting rule wouldn't work and wouldn't be chosen as the best rule over the period of a year.

It's a great rule for handling lumpy demand items such as spare parts. Spare parts sell very little month to month. For example: 0-1-0-0-0-0-8-0-1-0-0. The formula that we'll sell as many of this spare part in the next three months as what we did in the last three months is probably our best forecasting rule. During the energy crisis, when locking gas caps and siphon hoses were accelerating demand beyond belief, this little stalwart, "we'll probably sell what we sold in the last three months," was probably the be-all, end-all best possible way to forecast future sales of those energy-related products.

33

For those of you who can't bring yourself to use a forecast that says F=Q1, we'll probably sell what we sold the last three months, you can use exponential smoothing with an alpha factor of .5. That's the same as using "whatever we sold the last three months we'll probably sell the next three months." It sounds more clever when you explain it to someone, however.

In the world forecasting tournament a series of data was selected. Various forecasting rules were run against that series of data to find out which rule would work the best. This little rule "we'll probably sell what we sold the last three months" is what won. Of course, those were operations research people that were analyzing the accuracy of the techniques, so they said simple exponential smoothing won. But exponential smoothing with a high alpha factor is the same as saying we'll probably sell what we sold in the last three months.

The bottom line is, Don't think about using Focus Forecasting unless it includes "we'll probably sell whatever we sold in the last three months. F=Q1."

4. We'll probably sell 1/2 what we sold in the last 6 months.

Let F = the forecast.
Let Q1 = the most recent past 3 months.
Let Q2 = the 3 months before that.

The formula is $F = (Q1 + Q2) / 2$.

The worse the companies' demand history looks, the better this formula is for them.

A. There are random promotions in the demand history.
B. The item's sales or usage is very low or sporadic . . . 0-1-0-0-0-0-8-0-1-0-0.
C. The company captures shipment rather than demand history and often runs out of stock.
D. There is little or no seasonality in the business.
E. Very few major customers randomly order large quantities of goods.

F. The items are private-label and so the ordering is to
    discretion of a single customer.

The more random the demand history is, the better a longer-
term moving average is for a semireasonable forecast. Of course the
real answer is to correct the problems with the company's demand
history.

   5. Whatever % we are running versus last year on this item we
      will continue to run on this item.

      Let F = the forecast.
      Let Q1 = the most recent past 3 months.
      Let Q5 = the same 3 months last year.

      The formula is F = Q4* (Q1/Q5).

This is a useful formula for somewhat seasonal items. It's dangerous on highly seasonal items because the demand is so small in the
beginning of the season. Using this formula, it is usually best to put
a limit on the allowable increase this year versus last year.
   Another problem with this formula is what to do when last year
was zero for the past three months. Dividing the most recent past
three months by zero creates an infinite percent increase.

   6. Whatever we sold last month we will sell in the next 3 months.

      Let F = the forecast.
      Let M1 = the most recent month.

      The formula is F = M1.

This is a powerful formula for catching items that are dying.
Sometimes a company creates a new item that devastates another
item in its line. Or sometimes a fad just dies. Or sometimes the
circumstances creating demand for an item change. Some people
misunderstand this formula. It is not that in the next three months we

will sell three times as much as last month. It is in the next three months in total we will sell only what we sold last month.

7. We will sell what the salesman forecast.

Let F = the forecast.
Let S = the salesman's forecast.

The formula is F = S.

Sometimes there is someone in the company who greatly influences the sales of an item or group of items. Sometimes the best formula is to use that person's forecast.

Selecting Formulas for Your Company

Most companies start with just a sampling of their product line. There is no statistical way that we know of to analyze what group of formulas is best for a company with Focus Forecasting. We use simulation to find the best mix of formulas. Here's the procedure:

1. Select about two thousand items from the company's line of products. Of course, if the whole line is less than two thousand items, then the company might as well just run all the products.
2. Run Focus Forecasting over the time period that the company's most interested in forecasting accurately. If their ordering lead times, safety times, and review times occur over a period of three months, then the forecast accuracy horizon that they are most interested in would be three months. So all of your evaluations of forecast accuracy would run over a three-month period.
3. Recap the forecast accuracy. Of the two thousand items, how many items used:

Formula A We'll probably have the average company increase
Formula B We'll probably sell what we sold last year
Formula C We'll probably sell what we sold in the last 3 months

 # Of Items
With a Forecast Error of

Formula	< +70%	< +50%	< +30%	< +10%	<-10%	<-20%	<-30%	<-50%	<-70%	Total
A										
B										
C										
Etc										
Total										

Total algebraic dollar forecast error
Mean absolute dollar forecast error

The rows of the summary matrix in the evaluation of the forecast accuracy would be each of these formulas. The columns would be the forecast accuracy experienced—how many items were 70 percent low, 50 percent low, 30 percent low, etc. This histogram will tell the company with their beginning formulas what kind of forecast accuracy to expect and what would be the distribution of forecast accuracy. It would tell whether the company should expect overall to forecast low or high with this group of formulas.

4. Pick out the formula that had the highest incidence of forecast error. Try removing that formula from the set of formulas and resummarize the total network. If the overall accuracy has increased, keep that formula out of the formula mix; if it's decreased, put it back.

5. There will be some clusters of forecast inaccuracy. For example, maybe nineteen items show 70 percent low using formula B. Identify those items and play "Can You Outguess Focus Forecasting?" with your buyer or planner on those items. See if they have particular formulas that are effective.

6. Play "Can You Outguess Focus Forecasting?" on a random group of items with anyone involved with forecasting. It not only improves the selection of forecast formulas, but it makes believers of the people playing the game.

7. Include some of these formulas where the players were more effective than Focus Forecasting and rerun the overall summary to see if the forecast accuracy has improved or decreased. Keep doing these iterations until only marginal improvements or reduction in accuracy occur.

8 Narrow the number of formulas down to the fewest number of formulas for your company as possible. Using the fewest number of formulas greatly simplifies the use of Focus Forecasting, as people only have to be familiar with those formulas and it also speeds up the processing of the Focus Forecasting calculations.

Once a company has gone through this exercise it probably will never do it again unless the nature of the company's business changes completely. We used this procedure to select formulas for Servistar® Corporation back in 1972; that group of Focus Forecasting formulas is still running.

How a Formula Is Picked for an Item

To see how a formula is picked for an item, let's imagine a Focus Forecasting system where there are only two formulas. Here's the demand history by month last year and this year:
Here are the two formulas:
A. We'll probably sell what we sold last year.
$F = Q4$.
B. We'll probably sell what we sold in the last three months.
$F = Q1$.

Month	1	2	3	4	5	6	7	8	9	10	11	12
Demand History												
Last Year	1	0	6	1	2	7	17	11	5	24	13	0
This Year	4	12	0	1	13	0						

Imagine still further that we have only eighteen months of history: last year 1 through 12 and this year 1 through 6. We're sitting right at the end of month 6 this year, and we're trying to forecast months 7 through 9.

The first thing Focus Forecasting does is drop back a period of time in order to test the two formulas on the recent past. For example, here Focus Forecasting might drop back to month 3 and forecast months 4 through 6 using formula A: we'll probably sell what we sold last year. The answer would be 10.

Next Focus Forecasting forecasts months 4 through 6 using formula B: we'll probably sell what we sold in the last three months. The answer would be 16.

Focus Forecasting could at this point pick one of the two formulas based on which formula did the best in the recent past.

Forecast of Months 4 through 6

Formula	Result	Actual	Difference
A F = Q4	10	14	-4
B F = Q1	16	14	-2

Whichever forecast came the closest to forecasting 4 through 6, that's the formula Focus Forecasting would select to forecast months 7 through 9.

When Focus Forecasting tests these two formulas it doesn't just test whether or not they work the best on the last three months; it goes back as many iterations as the user specifies. Sometimes the best test for selecting a Focus Forecasting formula is a twelve-month iteration. This says what formula worked the best month by month for the whole year on this item. By picking the formula that worked the best for the whole year on the item, Focus Forecasting is able to select seasonal formulas for seasonal items and basic formulas for nonseasonal items.

Focus Forecasting uses this process whether there are two formulas or twenty formulas. That's why it's relatively useless to second-guess Focus Forecasting unless you know something about the data the system does not. The system has already tried all of the different methods of forecasting the item, and it has tried them for every month of a whole year period. No casual observation of the data should do a better job selecting a forecast rule.

Inventory management requires these detail item forecasts. What about forecasting total company sales dollars or product group summaries? Next is a discussion of aggregate sales forecasting related to Focus Forecasting.

Chapter Seven

Aggregate Forecasting Proration

Aggregate forecast prorations versus summaries of item sales forecasts: who is responsible for the item sales forecast?

1. When Things Are Going Well

It's a common practice these days to make marketing responsible for the item forecast. We make them own it. In other words, if they forecast low and we run out of stock, it's their fault. If they forecast high and we have excesses, it's their fault. If marketing is responsible for out-of-stocks and marketing is responsible for overstocks, what is the inventory management department responsible for? The answer is basically nothing.

Things have been going pretty well; the marketing department has been generating some pretty good sales increases year after year. They've had time to dabble in other things besides generating sales volume—advertising, doing market research, selecting new products, pricing and setting financial sales goals. They've had time to dabble in item forecasting. When things are going well they don't mind being responsible for the item forecast.

2. When Things Are Going Badly

Just picture yourself as the president of a company, and the year of the great recession is happening to your company. You go over to your marketing department and find them busily churning out numbers for the inventory management and production control departments. You ask them what they are doing in the office. Why aren't they out in the field selling something, or at least why aren't they thinking up new advertising campaigns, researching new products, or devising better pricing strategy? But they give you blank stares.

The marketing department is using the latest forecasting tools to produce reams of paper. They're circling numbers on those reams of paper, putting green circles on some and blue circles on others. They're breaking their dollar quotas down into individual items with weekly lumps of demand. They're checking their forecast error and jumping on problems that have tracking signals flashing *error, error!*

Again you ask, "Why are sales off?" The marketing department gives you an item-by-item breakdown of where sales have been less than forecast. "But what are you doing about it?" you ask, and they say, "Oh, we're revising our forecasts."

Well, when things are going badly that scenario would last about one day. After that it's marketing department back to their primary job: generating volume for the company; item sales forecasting back to the inventory-management production control ranks.

Sales and Marketing

Marketing should be responsible for setting the total dollar sales goals for company expense planning.

Sales and Marketing, as the terms denote, have a primary responsibility to generate sales volume. Marketing is the intelligence side of sales, helping with market research information, advertising, pricing strategies, and deployment of the sales force. Marketing can and should give input to the item forecast. They know when they are going to run an upcoming promotion. They know when they are going to cut prices on an item. They know when they will have a group of product specials for the month. They know the start and end dates of the deal periods. They should be held accountable for communicating this information as accurately as possible to the inventory management division of the company.

If that's done slovenly or sloppily, sales and marketing should be penalized for not providing input in a professional manner. But the job of forecasting the everyday sales of thousands of items in the company is primarily based on historical data, and the responsibility for those forecasts belongs in the inventory management group. The

42

person who gets fired for too many out-of-stocks or too slow an inventory turnover, chaos in the work flow, or loss of gross profit because of dumping excesses or missing potential big buys is the one who should be responsible if forecasts are grossly in error on a continuing basis. Who else can raise the flag that marketing is giving poor input? Who else can make the judgments on the day-to-day forecasting of the company's hundreds and thousands of products?

Management

In most companies if you ask, "Who gets fired if we run out of stock of too many items?" there is no answer. And if you ask, "Who gets fired if the inventory excesses start to run us out of business?" no one can point a finger. The old term for the person responsible for this job was *inventory manager.* He's the one responsible for the customer service, the turnover, the amount of work the systems are generating, and the maintained gross profit because of inventory excesses and volume buying. The new term for the inventory manager is *director of logistics.* It's not a job to make things right, it's a job to make sure the company has the right things in the right quantities at the right time.

The Procedure

The person responsible for the item forecast must be the person responsible for being in stock and not being overstocked. This person **should be measured on their accuracy and timeliness in providing this** this data. They should be measured against their sales goals. But they must not be held responsible for individual forecasts of repeat-item sales. They don't know what the sales are going to be!

After the logistics person has made an item forecast using Focus items, price changes, flyers, radio and TV advertising. Marketing should be measured on their accuracy and timelines in providing this data. They should be measured against their sales goals. But they must not be held responsible for individual forecasts of repeat-item sales. They don't know what the sales are going to be!

After the logistics person has made an item forecast using Focus Forecasting, the total company forecast can be aggregated in dollars and compared to the company financial plan. There are real reasons for differences. Don't use the dead-brain approach of proportioning the difference to all of the items.

Reasons for Differences between the Item Forecast and the Company Plan

1. Companies don't ship 100 percent of their customers' orders! The item forecast should normally be 5 to 15 percent higher than the company financial forecast.
2. All of the new items for the coming year have zero sales history, and therefore Focus Forecasting is forecasting too low.
3. Many of the items Focus Forecasting is forecasting will be discontinued, so Focus Forecasting is forecasting too high.
4. Usually item demand histories are not reduced for returns. So item forecasts will be higher than financial forecasts.
5. Marketing will special-price and promote some items they did not promote last year.
6. We are losing a customer whom we used to sell private-label.
7. The item demand history has garbage in it. One item alone is forecasting sales of $10 million.
8. This is the year we are going to dump our excess inventory.
9. Manufacturing doesn't have the capacity to support the item sales forecast.
10. We are phasing out of plastic and moving to biodegradables.
11. The sales budget is always understated to keep pressure on expenses.
12. The sales budget is always overstated to make the salesmen aim high.

When we are done with reconciliation, the pure item forecast will not add up to the financial forecast. The only way it can add up is if we force it to be wrong. There should be summary figures that explain the difference between the item forecast and the financial forecast. But please don't fix the item forecast to make it add up perfectly to the financial forecast.

Forecasting by Distribution Center versus Global Forecasts

Most companies start their production planning by forecasting an item's sales for the total company, disregarding the fact that they are stocked in various distribution centers. They usually have the plants produce against the item sales to the customer for the total company. They are usually shocked to find that they have constant problems throughout the year, as the individual distribution centers draw from the plants' quantities that don't add up to the global customer forecasts.

The sum of the distribution centers planned orders to restock their warehouses will just about never equal the global forecasts of customer sales for the company. There are a lot of possible reasons for this:

1. The inventory is imbalanced. Some distribution centers have over-stock of an item and won't replenish any for the whole year; others are out of stock from day one.
2. Some distribution centers will be increasing their inventories in order to reduce their customer service problems.
3. Other distribution centers may be reducing their inventories to try to get out of warehouse space problems and financial investment problems.
4. Some distribution centers will order more of an item than they need in order to head off a possible shortage situation they antici-pate in the future. Sometimes by ordering these extra stocks they actually create the shortage position.
5. Some distribution centers will order truckloads of goods in order to reduce freight costs and handling even though they have no immediate need for the stock.

For all of these reasons, producing or purchasing against total customer sales for a company in situations where companies have multiple distribution centers rarely works. The proper way to forecast is to forecast the item sales at the distribution-center level and use Distribution Resource Planning to match the distribution center sales against the existing inventories in the distribution centers and the existing scheduled receipts in the distribution centers. The resulting planned orders should be summed up to present gross requirements to the company's master production schedule.

Any other procedure automatically creates inventory imbalances, chaos, phone calls, and rushed freight. Of course, 90 percent of the companies in the world produce against global customer forecasts even though they have multiple distribution centers, because DRP is a relatively new concept.

Here's a company producing against a global customer forecast versus a company producing against the sum of the planned orders from a DRP system. It shows that not only should a company forecast at the item level, but the company should forecast at the item-distribution-center level.

By the end of the first four weeks of the production plan a company that planned against a global customer forecast in this example would be short 112 pieces even with a 100 percent accurate forecast! (See illustration on page 47.)

Forecasting by Customer

It's worthwhile from a marketing standpoint to use Focus Forecasting to forecast customer sales for the coming year. The marketing manager can look at these forecasts versus goals that he has established for customer sales with significant accounts. If an account is large enough, however, to warrant forecasting at the item level, that item forecast should be done by the customer rather than the supplier. Only the customer knows when he will be offering an item at off price. Only the customer knows his existing on-hand on an item. Only the customer knows if he will be increasing or decreasing inventory of an item, and only the customer knows if he will be replacing this item with a substitute from an alternate supplier.

Focus Forecasting is a procedure for forecasting sku item sales from our company. If we get to the point though where we are trying to forecast customer purchases from us by item, the alternative should be to work with the customer to get schedules of the customer's planned orders going out into the future even if we have to pay the customer for the information!

Planning Production for Global
Customer Forecasts

Versus

Using DRP Planned Order Summaries
of Distribution Centers

Month

Dist Center	On Hand	Past Due	1	2	3	4	5	6	7	8	9	10	11	12
			Sales											
A	40		10	10	10	10	10	10	10	10	10	10	10	10
B	0		20	20	20	20	20	20	20	20	20	20	20	20
Imaginary Global Reqs		0	0	20	30	30	30	30	30	30	30	30	30	30

DRP Planned Orders *
(what the DCs will need from the plant)

Dist Center		Past Due	1	2	3	4	5	6	7	8	9	10	11	12
A		0	0	24	0	24	0	0	24	0	24	0	0	24
B		24	48	24	24	24	24	24	0	24	24	24	24	24
Real Future Global Reqs		24	48	48	24	48	24	24	24	24	48	24	24	48

* Safety Time 1.5 Weeks   In-transit Lead Time 1.0 Week   Ship Carton 24

Forecasting by Territory

Sometimes a company's sales territories will not match its distribution centers. So one sales territory will overlap two or three individual distribution centers. Right up front the best thing to do is to set up the territories so that no one territory is serviced by more than one distribution center. One distribution center can service multiple sales territories. The problem occurs when companies ask sales managers to break down territorial sales by distribution center.

In other words, simplify the distribution-center–sales-territory relationship as much as possible. Ideally, sales territories should be subsets of distribution centers. If a company can't change from territories selling from multiple distribution centers, they are faced with the problem of aggregating the item forecasts by territory in order to get marketing input by territory and then faced with the additional problem of breaking out the territorial sales in order to aggregate them for the individual distribution centers. This guarantees an additional 20 percent error in the marketing distribution center aggregate forecast.

Sales Aggregation

Dist Center	Territory 1	2	3	4	5	6	Total
A	X		X				No Problem
B		X		X			A Problem
C				X		X	A Problem

When the territory and distribution centers are set up correctly, Focus Forecasting can be a tremendous aid to the marketing department in disciplining their sales planning. It can help them use historic data to project future sales. It can become a vehicle for incorporating their judgment on sales promotions and special price offerings.

Reconciling the Differences

Once Focus Forecasting has made the individual item forecast based on history, Focus Forecasting can add up these item forecasts in dollars by family, by distribution center, by territory, and by total company. This aggregation creates a total company forecast. It's of value to compare this forecast based on historical data with the company's upcoming financial plan for sales. The differences allow the company to head off problems before they occur.

In reconciling the differences between the Focus Forecasting item forecast and the aggregate forecast a company never should automatically prorate the differences. Each difference should be carefully analyzed before changes are made either at the detail level or at the aggregate level. The process of analyzing these differences is in itself of value.

Tying Focus Forecasting into the Salesman's Forecast

One time I sat on a USAir flight from Pittsburgh to Florida. In the seat next to me a salesman had a stack of fourteen-by-eleven-inch data-processing computer printout. The computer printout had items and item descriptions listed by customer, and the salesman was feverishly filling in: 10, 10, 10, 10, 10, 10, 10, 20, 20, 20, 20, 20, 20, 20, 0 20, 0 20, 0 20, 0 20. I asked him what he was doing. What he was doing was preparing his customer forecast by item for his company. He had been given ownership of the forecast. He had no more idea of the accuracy of what he was doing than the man in the moon. After that I made careful note as I walked up and down the aisles of other airplanes to see whether or not there were other salesmen doing the same thing.

Here I found another salesman who had a fourteen-by-eleven-inch data-processing report printout with items, descriptions, and forecasts and he had a green pen, a red pen, and a yellow pen. He would circle some items with the red pen, strike out some figures with the green pen, and write in some figures with the yellow pen.

What was he doing? He said normally he didn't have to do this to the company forecast because normally he gave it to his eleven-year-old son to do for him and paid him two dollars. Once again, he had been given ownership of the forecast. It would only be by the wildest chance that he improved the computer-driven forecast that he was given.

Salesmen should not forecast by item unless they are selling big, big tickets, ten thousand dollars and up. Usually the most detail a salesman should forecast is dollars by customer, by family. The totals by family should be compared against the Focus Forecasting item forecast. Salesmen can forecast families by customer. Here is firm ground. Focus Forecasting can help them by keeping a history of family sales by customer and by doing initial projections of upcoming sales by family, by customer. But a salesman should almost never forecast by customer, by item. If that's required, ideally the salesmen should get the forecast from the customer.

Ideally that customer should provide that forecast by running Distribution Resource Planning on his data in order to provide a projection of planned orders to his supplier. It would be far better for a supplier to pay a customer for this information than to bother his sales force at all with the idiocy of trying to have the salesman forecast a customer by item.

Accuracy of Aggregating Time Periods

Accuracy improves when we forecast larger buckets. But the time period we should forecast—daily, weekly, or monthly buckets—should be in line with our inventory management decisions. If our ship packs or production runs are six months' supply it's ridiculous to forecast in days. If we are scheduling shipments of cigarettes or ice cream in half-day shifts we should be forecasting in days.

Generally speaking, the time interval that we should forecast—daily, weekly, or monthly—is a function of how often we review for replenishment, how long it takes to get that replenishment order, how many weeks' or months' supply we must make or buy at one time, and how much safety time we are willing to invest in the inventory to cover forecast errors.

Practically speaking, now it's a dead issue, because most forecasting systems forecast in months. Usually the DRP or MRP system prorates the monthly forecast into weeks or days, taking into account daily curves during the month peculiar to the company.

Detail Item Forecast or Proration

Early in my career I was in the girdle and bra business. I worked for Warner's World Famous Girdles and Bras. One of the fringe benefits in my career was watching the models show off the new lingerie fashions. When I started looking at the lingerie as products of our business and stopped looking at the models I knew it was time to

50

leave that industry. But while I was there I learned some interesting things. In bras there's a lot of sizing. Cup sizes run from AA's to DD's. Back sizes run from 24 to 46. So the combination of cup sizes and back sizes create for any given style of bra almost 32 skus. It was common practice when forecasting bras to use prorations in order to break down the individual sizes. Unfortunately, there were different styles of bras—underwires, contours, padded. Some styles of bras fit some sizes better than others. So using a proration to forecast the sales was a disaster.

One problem was that we almost always had most of our leftover in the AA's, DD's, 24s, and 46s. Even the sizing within the style was never distributed as we planned for in the ratios. As I think back, it would have been much better to forecast by style, cup, color, and size rather than to try to forecast at the style level and use any kind of preset ratio to break the forecast into individual stock-keeping units. This ratio procedure causes the fact that when you go into any store where there's leftover specials on sale you'll always notice that the extra smalls and the extra larges are always the greatest overstock on sales. The fact of the matter is that the middle sizes far outsell the extreme sizes in a proportion so large that no ratio formulation would be bold enough to allocate the sales properly. Whenever there is a choice, forecast by individual stock-keeping unit rather than forecasting by aggregate and prorating the answers.

Paperless Forecast Management

Most inventory management disasters that we've witnessed usually involve reams of data processing reports on fourteen-by-eleven-inch continuous forms. There is a mistaken notion that as long as the information is available it should be printed. Information is only of value if it changes a person's decision. If a forecasting system is hooked into a resource planning system, the only information that is of value to the planner or buyer is when the combination of the forecasts and resource planning is creating either out-of-stocks or overstocks. In 90 percent of the cases either the overstocks have already been created and nothing can be done about it or the system is operating as it was intended, ordering in a timely fashion and in reasonable quantities. Why print all of this information out in reams of paper? We even have clients who produce continuous forms who are delighted with paperless inventory management.

In a paperless system only forecasts that are creating overstocks or understocks are presented to the planner or buyer for review. The reams of paper stacking three and four feet high are no longer needed. At home we have television sets, video games, and video recorders. Isn't it time that our forecasting systems caught up to the pace in our leisure life and we stopped using wheelbarrows to cart our data-processing forecasting and inventory management reports from one office to the other?

In a paperless system we can forecast at the distribution-item level and without ever printing any results we can aggregate on a microprocessing screen and compare it against financial figures and territorial forecasts. Even if Focus Forecasting were not as accurate as it is, the discipline of being able to aggregate individual item forecasts and compare against company financial and marketing systems is a discipline well worth doing on a personal computer. The marvel of the personal computer is that in the paperless environment it allows the company to simulate various what-if scenarios to understand the difference between the detail item forecast and the aggregate company numbers.

Aggregate Forecasts with Proration or Detail Item Sales Forecasts

Let Marketing and Sales be responsible for the financial goals and projections, but let the person responsible for being in stock and not being overstocked be responsible for the item forecast. Let Marketing provide item information not indicated by the sales history and measure it on its timeliness and accuracy, but don't make them own the item sales forecast.

Use Focus Forecasting and history to forecast at the item level. Use Focus Forecasting to sum the item forecasts in dollars. Reconcile the difference, but don't force the detail forecasts to match the financial forecasts without sound analysis. Better not to do it at all than to just run a simple arithmetic proration.

This chapter suggests relying heavily on the accuracy of Focus Forecasting using historical data. What level of accuracy can you expect?

52

Chapter Eight

Focus Forecasting Accuracy

What Level of Accuracy to Expect

The accuracy to expect is that Focus Forecasting will project more accurately than the existing forecasting system. Beware of evaluating any forecasting system based on some imaginary percentage error criteria. Resist decisions based on "aesthetically the forecast looks lousy" or "let's remove from the demand history the nonforecastable items." Just because the forecasting system is off 50 percent on some items doesn't mean it's bad. Without that forecasting system perhaps some people would be off 100 percent. All forecasts are wrong. The percentage errors are usually much more extraordinary than people would want to believe, especially people with accounting backgrounds, who are used to debits equaling credits and inventory record accuracy being in the 99 percent range. They usually say something like "the forecast is acceptable if it has no more than a 20 percent error."

Only God can set acceptable percentage errors on forecasting. The only thing companies can do is install forecasting systems that are more accurate than what they have been using in the past. Understandably, the percentage errors will be higher in forecasting very low-demand items like spare parts and the forecast error will be lower in forecasting things like diapers, tires, and two-inch carriage bolts. In the table you see the ranking of products with highest forecast accuracy to lowest forecast accuracy expected.

These are the expected errors on individual item forecasts on the average.

Type of Item	Forecast Error Expected		
	Manufacturing	Wholesaling	Retailing
Lumpy Demand	150%	200%	300%
Highly Seasonal	75%	100%	150%
Disaster-related	75%	100%	175%
Basic Items	15%	25%	50%

Measuring Forecast Accuracy

The Old Way: Item MADS and SADS

My friend Herman Separack and I were wiring control panels at Warner's World Famous Girdles and Bras when we first met Bob Brown. We were trying to use exponential smoothing to forecast the various styles of bras and girdles in the various colors, cups, and sizes. He explained to us how to sum the algebraic deviations in the forecast errors. We would just subtract the actual from the forecast, and whatever the difference was, we would keep a running total. He explained to us how to keep an average of the absolute errors. All we did was keep a six-month average of the absolute forecast error. As I recall, we even used exponential smoothing in order to get the six-month average absolute forecast error.

Then he told us to divide the average absolute error into the sum of the algebraic errors. With that old unit record equipment we had to move over to a 602 A in order to do the division because the 402 tabulator could only add and subtract, but it couldn't divide. "The result," Bob said, "is a tracking signal. If it's any number higher than 4, list out those items as a separate group. If it's a plus 4, you know that your forecast is very bad and high. If it's a minus 4, you know your forecast is very bad and low."

Well, we did all that faithfully with our unit record equipment

Mean Absolute Deviation Calculation

	Forecast Demand	Actual Demand	Algebraic Deviation	Absolute Deviation
Jan	123	142	-19	19
Feb	119	157	-38	38
Mar	120	80	+40	40
Apr	97	108	-11	11
May	105	387	-282	282
Jun	135	34	+101	101
Tot	699	908	-209	491

Tracking Signal = $(-209)/(491/6) = -2.55$

and prepared lists of items that had forecast errors that fell outside of the tracking signals. Once we had those, we would stare at the number and empirically change it to something that seemed reasonable. We didn't have any more data than the machine had, but we could tell from some of the weird answers exponential smoothing came up with that there was no chance in this world that the exponential smoothing forecast would happen.

Probably with exponential forecasting approaches that come up with totally unreasonable forecasts using mean absolute deviations and tracking signals is a good way to kick out item forecast errors. With Focus Forecasting every forecast is possible and reasonable based on the past. Whether the tracking signal is 1, 2, 3, 4, 5, or 9 really doesn't matter, because with the existing data a person could not make a more reasonable forecast anyway.

Bob Brown's wife at that time, Inge Brown, reviewed Focus Forecasting in her newsletter. She said that it was total rubbish and the only reason it worked at all was because of our management skill at American Hardware. She had promised us that after her editorial was okayed for publication she would give us equal space for a rebuttal. In our rebuttal we asked to visit any installation in the world where they were forecasting all of the items using exponential smoothing and using 95 percent of the results without change.

As Ollie Wight said to us, "Exponential smoothing users are like chickens in a barnyard. After laying eggs for so many years, they should look around at each other and ask, 'Why aren't there more of us?'"

She never did publish our rebuttal. We just did.

Some More on Item Tracking Signals

The theory behind tracking signals is that if a forecast becomes unreasonable the data should be displayed to the user so the user can make a more reasonable forecast. Focus Forecasting doesn't make unreasonable forecasts if the demand history is sound. So the only tracking signal that might be of value is a tracking signal that evaluates the reasonability of the demand. Once demand has been aggregated by item it's very difficult to tell whether the demand is reasonable or not. The place to catch unreasonable demand, the place for tracking signals to kick out unreasonable demand, is at the customer-item level.

When your customer orders seven Mercedes-Benz engines instead of seven Mercedes-Benz spark plugs, that's the time to ask the customer whether he really wants the engines; that's the time for the tracking signal to kick out the unreasonable demand.

Measuring Forecast Accuracy

Above we mentioned that the traditional approach for measuring forecast accuracy is tracking signals . . . the sum of the algebraic deviations divided by the mean absolute deviation. There is a basic flaw with evaluating forecasting systems by looking at individual item forecasts. All forecasts are wrong. How can you tell from looking at the forecast of an individual item whether or not the formula is wrong for the company as a whole? And again, if you do tailor a formula to a specific item will it work for other items?

Tracking signals are not of much value for individual items. But for total company measurement of forecast accuracy the concepts of mean absolute deviation and sum of the algebraic deviations are significant indicators. If we add up all of the algebraic deviations for the entire company's product line—in other words, subtract the actual from the forecast for every item and sum all of the differences—that summary number is significant. If it shows a high negative number, then overall, the system is forecasting low. If it shows a high positive number overall, the system is forecasting high.

Caution: Do the summary in value. Otherwise the company may have some items that sell hundreds of thousands and other items that only sell ten or twenty. One error on an item that sells one hundred thousand can bias the whole summary measure. In those cases it's better to extend the forecast error either in value or some other unit that weights the relative forecast accuracy. The sum of the dollarized algebraic deviations for all of the items in the company is a good indicator of the forecast accuracy of the company's total system.

The other concept is the mean absolute deviation. By adding up all of the deviations without regard to sign of all of the items and dividing by the number of items in the product line we get a mean absolute deviation. This average error tells us the magnitude of the forecasting errors that we are experiencing. The sum of the algebraic deviations and the mean absolute deviation are both good concepts when looking at product lines as a group. As stated above, they're not of much significance when measuring individual item's performance.

Histograms

A very useful technique for evaluating forecast accuracy is to show the number of forecasts distributed by forecast error and by formula. In other words, if we have ten formulas A through J, recap the forecast error by how many forecasts were 70 percent or more low, 50 percent or more low, 30 percent or more low, 10 percent or more low, 10 percent or more high, 30 percent or more high, 50 percent or more high, 70 percent or more high. Use a summary

Old System
of Items
(forecast-actual)/actual

Formula	<-70%	<-50%	<-30%	<-10%	<+10%	<+30%	<+50%	<+70%	>+70%	Total
X	40	21	45	52	87	48	27	14	105	439

59% of items within + or - 50%
69% of items within + or - 70%

Focus Forecasting
# of Items
(forecast-actual)/actual

Formula	<-70%	<-50%	<-30%	<-10%	<+10%	<+30%	<+50%	<+70%	>+70%	Total
3	0	0	0	1	0	0	0	0	0	1
4	3	4	2	4	8	5	2	1	6	35
6	3	4	8	4	6	5	2	3	9	44
7	15	7	15	19	26	10	8	5	10	115
13	8	8	17	12	25	21	6	10	19	126
15	0	2	0	5	13	5	2	8	11	46
16	0	2	6	9	19	12	5	2	16	71
21	0	0	0	0	1	0	0	0	0	1
Total	29	27	48	54	98	58	25	29	71	439

64% of items within + or - 50%
77% of items within + or - 70%

matrix to make sure the new system in total is better than your old system.

This histogram is a great way to evaluate your existing forecast procedure versus Focus Forecasting and also a great way to select Focus Forecasting formulas to add to or delete from the Focus Forecasting vocabulary of possible forecast formulas.

1. Select a time period to evaluate the forecast accuracy. A good time period is whatever time period is critical to your inventory management decision. For example, a company that reviews inventory once a week, carries three weeks of safety time, and has an average replenishment lead time of nine weeks has a decision period of about three months. Their critical forecast accuracy period would be about three months. They should select the system that is most accurate in forecasting the last three months of history.
2. Run the summary analysis for your old method of forecasting versus Focus Forecasting for the three-month period that is already history. See which is better.
3. Eliminate one formula at a time to see whether Focus Forecasting accuracy improves or gets worse as you proceed. Use the summary analysis as a criterion.
4. Play "Can You Outguess the Computer Forecast?" with the users to find possible new formulas to add to the system. Use the summary analysis as a criterion.

The histogram shows which formulas reflect the most error and show whether a forecast is biased high or low. By looking at a particular row and column we can see how many items were using formula 7, for example, and were more than 50 percent off. Using the histogram approach we can then take all of the items that fell within that row and column and analyze the actual forecast versus actual. This can be done most effectively by playing "Can You Outguess Focus Forecasting?" on these items to see if there is any effective technique that might have forecast these items more efficiently. If there is a more efficient procedure, perhaps that formula could be added to Focus Forecasting and the formula that was not working could be deleted from Focus Forecasting. Then the histogram could be run over again to see whether overall forecast accuracy improved or deteriorated.

Aggregate Dollar Forecast Error Measures

One measure we like in particular is to show the aggregate dollar forecast for all of the items in the population out month by month into the future—to show the same projection one under the other so that, for instance, if we were forecasting in December we would have six forecasts for the month of July and then finally July's actual. This aggregate measure of forecast error handily shows how much error is in the forecast depending on how far out in the future you are forecasting.

In aggregates we don't see as much of a problem with summing the total algebraic deviations in dollars and dividing by the average absolute deviation in order to get a tracking system for the whole. As your company moves in and out of economic recoveries and economic recessions this total tracking signal shows how your system is performing. (See illustration on page 62.)

Family Rules of Thumb

Just by a rule of thumb companies know that white paint outsells green paint. A company can add up all of the item forecasts in the white paint family and all of the forecasts in the green paint family. The white paint should outsell green paint in the order of about 8 to 1. Suppose it doesn't. Suppose the white forecasts only equal the green paint forecasts. That should be a tip-off that the individual white paint items are not all accounted for or there's something wrong with the white paint demand data. On the other hand, perhaps there's something wrong with the green paint item demand data; perhaps there's some erroneous spike of demand in there causing a false inflated projection.

Family rules of thumb are good ways to assess the detailed item forecast at the aggregate level. Family mix percentages of total business rarely change dramatically in a short period of time. If there is a certain percentage mix of housewares, sporting goods, paint and paint products, heating, fasteners, lawn and garden tools, and electrical, that percentage mix relationship should not change dramatically

Month by Month
Forecast versus Actual
in $1,000,000

Jun XXXX

Forecast	Jan	Feb	Mar	Apr	May	Jun	Jul	Aug	Sep	Oct	Nov	Dec
Jan	*96	107	134	234	321	132	204					
Feb		*112	127	216	324	140	211	189				
Mar			*113	205	317	127	198	176	205			
Apr				*215	318	130	201	183	214	178		
May					*353	156	234	218	278	201	176	
Jun						*148	212	197	234	185	165	101

* actual company sales in $1,000,000 for all items

Annual Sales Volume
Versus
Annual Forecast Volume

Family	Actual	% Mix	Forecast	% Mix
Housewares	$21,230	11	$24,100	10
Sporting Goods	13,510	7	21,690	9
Paint Products	19,300	10	19,280	8
Lumber	7,720	4	4,820	2
Fasteners	17,370	9	26,510	11
Lawn & Garden	34,740	18	50,610	21
Tools	28,950	15	31,330	3
Electrical	17,370	9	19,280	8
Plumbing	15,440	8	24,100	10
Heating	17,370	9	19,280	8
Total $	$193,000	100	$241,000	100

in the upcoming current forecasts. If it does, there's probably something wrong with an individual item data demand history. There's an illustration of family percentage distributions of total business on page 63.

Can You Outguess Focus Forecasting?

The most effective way to make people believe and trust in Focus Forecasting is to play "Can You Outguess Focus Forecasting?" with them. Take one of your items. Take the demand history for the past twenty-four months. Back up six months and pretend those six months didn't happen. Then get three or four people from your company. Let them see the same demand history that Focus Forecasting sees. Let them try to forecast the next three months' demand. Compare their results with the results of Focus Forecasting.

If they win, if their forecast comes closer to the actual than Focus Forecasting, ask them how they forecast. More than likely a company can add whatever formula they were using to its Focus Forecasting vocabulary of formulas. If a company adds a user's personal formula to its vocabulary of Focus Forecasting formulas, that sells that user forever. However, never add a user's formula simply because it outguessed an individual item. The only time to add an individual formula is when it improves the forecast accuracy of all of the items in the company in total.

A formula might say, "Whatever we sold last month we'll sell next month." It might work just great for an individual item at this moment in time. But adding that formula to the vocabulary of Focus Forecasting formulas may very well reduce the accuracy of Focus Forecasting over all the items over a period of time.

When we play "Can You Outguess Focus Forecasting?" with people sometimes they forecast better than Focus Forecasting and sometimes they forecast worse. They always learn that Focus Forecasting makes reasonable forecasts based on the demand data that's available. That's important . . . Focus Forecasting always makes reasonable forecasts. Look at the forecasts of the people on stage: Lisa guessed 39, Mike guessed 20, Shirley guessed 75, and Focus Forecasting guessed 39. If you changed the system's name to Frank or Francis no one could distinguish Focus Forecasting's guess of what will happen from that of any of the people on stage.

Can You Outguess Focus Forecasting?

Dandelion Digger

Last Yr	51	163	568	340	107	46	25	4	10	0	0	15
This Yr	37	113	205	488	142	48	?	?	?			
Lisa	39											
Mike	20											
Shirley	75											
FF	39											

*for the answer see page 239 Focus Forecasting Computer Techniques for Inventory Control

Is Focus Forecasting More Accurate than Other Systems?

There *are* other forecasting systems. Most all of them are based on R. G. Brown's exponential smoothing. Some of them are esoteric systems. Only a very select number of brilliant people know how they work. Most of them require considerable study to understand how they operate. Are they worth it? Will Focus Forecasting outperform these systems? There's no doubt in our minds that in the hundreds of companies that we've worked with in reviewing forecasting systems Focus Forecasting will outforecast any statistical approach to forecasting the future if the demand data are reasonable. Demand data are reasonable if formulas that worked in the recent past to forecast what happened will work in the future to forecast what will happen. If the demand data are not reasonable then simple averages are the best forecasters of future demand. Of course in those companies priority one is not a new forecasting system. It should be "fix the demand history."

If the data are such that they display any sort of continuing pattern where the recent past is some indication of what will work in the future, Focus Forecasting will outperform any statistical model on the order of 10 to 15 percent. It will outperform even manual guesses of the future on the order of 5 to 10 percent.

There is one other case where Focus Forecasting will be outperformed by statistical models. Where college professors create data that has built into it observable statistical trends, seasonality, and cycles, those data of course fit better the statistical models that are forecasting them. In those events Focus Forecasting will not outperform the statistical system and if the data is tailored well enough to the statistical system the statistical system will outperform Focus Forecasting. But in just about every normal company in the world with demand data that is an expression of customers ordering what they need, Focus Forecasting will outperform any existing statistical technique and probably any future statistical technique.

By "statistical technique" we mean techniques that rely on normal distributions, that rely on actual patterns of seasonality, cycles, and averages.

In addition, Focus Forecasting will forecast all of the items in a company's line, the A, B, C, and D items. It will outperform statistical techniques on the A item to some degree, and it will dramatically outperform statistical techniques in the B, C, and D items.

Do not take our word for it. Use the histogram approach to evaluate any new forecasting system selection for your company.

What level of accuracy should you expect? Demand a level of accuracy in any new system including Focus Forecasting that is superior to the accuracy of your existing forecasting system. One of the primary reasons forecasts are not more accurate is that the demand histories they are based on are unsound. The next chapter talks about capturing good demand histories.

Chapter Nine

Creating Sound Demand Histories

Here is a picture of the ideal demand for an item:

1. Twenty-four to forty-two months of history.
2. A summary of customer orders by month.
3. The customer can order whenever the customer needs goods without a penalty.

Here are some of the problems companies have in their item histories. Many they create with their own policy:

1. There is only one year of history available.
2. The history is not recorded by individual month or week.
3. The history is not recorded at the distribution-center level.
4. The company encourages orders for future shipment.
5. The order entry system does not challenge unusual order quantities at the customer-item level.
6. Customers order and return things they don't need to make minimum order or shipment quantity freight prepaid or bonuses.
7. There is only a history of what the company was able to ship rather than what the customer ordered.
8. The shipment history shows zero orders on out-of-stock items.
9. The shipment figures are inflated when the company pushes to meet year-end budgets.
10. The company does not backorder, and repeat orders for out-of-stock items are counted as multiple orders.
11. The salesman or customer calls in to see if goods are available before placing orders.
12. The company offers promotions or discounts or advertises items at random times during the year.

13. The company does not separate orders from customers from orders to replenish its own warehouses.
14. The company has manually tampered with the demand history so much that it is unreliable.

Demand History

Most companies that have computer forecasting systems use monthly buckets of demand history. Focus Forecasting can start forecasting with as little as one month's history. Of course, it will always select the formula "we'll probably sell next month what we sold last month." With nine months of history it can start to choose "we'll probably sell what we sold in the last three months" or "we'll probably sell half as much as we did in the last six months." It's not until it actually has eighteen months of demand history that it can start to choose seasonal formulas such as "we'll probably sell what we sold last year" or "we'll probably have the average company increase" or "we'll probably continue to have the average increase over last year on this item that we've had so far this year on this item."

There is a break-even point for a company where the benefits of using the recent past outweigh adding more past demand history to an item's forecast record. But to measure a seasonal formula properly versus all other formulas requires at least two years of history. If there were two calendar years, for example, Focus Forecasting would use formulas to forecast January through March of the most recent year, February through April of the most recent year, etc., all the way through October through December. Since it tests a selection of formulas on every quarter for the year, if the item is seasonal it will choose a seasonal formula.

Focus Forecasting could use as much as five years of history. It could find the formula that worked the best for an item over a five-year period. Once it starts going back further than two years, however, it is testing using ancient history and may no longer be using the formula that worked the best in the recent past. Formulas that worked best in the recent past are those most likely to work in the future.

So the demand history for Focus Forecasting should at least be about two years in an average company. This doesn't mean that a company should wait two years to install a Focus Forecasting system. Focus Forecasting will work on whatever data is available, from one month forward.

Some companies have demand history going back two years in a global total by item but don't have it for individual distribution centers. As a start-up procedure it is possible to use a proration to break up global history into individual distribution center item history. It's the best approximation right now that a company has of its prior demand history. As the real demand history starts to feed into the Focus Forecasting system it will choose strategies in relation to the prorated demand history that do start to accurately forecast the future. That's one of the beauties of the Focus Forecasting system—it doesn't depend on statistical consistency. Even in a crooked game where a company wrongly prorated the previous demand history Focus Forecasting will begin to lock in on the formulas that do forecast the future.

In other words, suppose the company prorated too low a demand for a specific item in the past. Suppose the current demand started to come in at higher levels than the prior history would indicate. Focus Forecasting would start to use formulas that expressed percentage increases over the prior data or short moving average periods. It's almost like magic.

Similarly if a company switches over from shipment history to demand history Focus Forecasting will choose strategies that bridge the gap as well as possible between the conversion from shipments to demand. Even if a company has a situation where prior demand patterns included random promotion offerings, Focus Forecasting will start to use the new corrected demand patterns efficiently. If nothing else is available, the best thing to start with is just whatever the past month's history was.

If only annual demand is available for an item, it is worthwhile to curve that annual demand so that it approximates what the expected seasonality of the item was. This curving strategy is of value in starting up Focus Forecasting on items that have been in the company's line for many years but where only annual demand history has been accumulated. It's not of value for brand-new items. If a company curves a seasonal demand pattern for new items, the company will cause more forecast error than it corrects. New items follow a distribution cycle. New items do not follow their normal seasonality in their first year of introduction.

So collect a two-year monthly demand history for Focus Forecasting. If your company needs to approximate to get the monthly distribution of demand over that two-year history, as the new real monthly demand history develops Focus Forecasting will move to formulas that accurately forecast the future for this item.

Orders for Future Shipment

Orders for future shipment mean different things to a manufacturer, to a wholesaler, to a retailer, and to a supplier of spare parts to an industry.

1. Manufacturers

Manufacturing companies can either produce to stock, produce to order, or do both. Manufacturers often offer special incentives to their customers to place orders for future delivery. These orders for future shipment complicate matters when considering a forecast horizon. For instance, if we forecast January, February, and March, but we already have in hand customer orders for future delivery on February 15, are the orders for future shipment part of the forecast or should they be added to the forecast?

1. If the orders for future shipment are in the item's demand history, the right approach is to use the sum of the orders in house for future shipment or the mechanical forecast, whichever is higher. (We credit this concept to Bill Todd of Avery International.)
2. If the orders for future shipment are not in the item's demand history, the right approach is to add the orders for future shipment to the mechanical forecast as a special requirement.

A company should ask, What is the purpose of the order for future shipment in the first place? Generally speaking, customers issue orders for future delivery for one or more of the following reasons:

1. The supplier offers a discount to the customer for the order for future shipment.
2. The supplier makes a delivery guarantee in exchange for the order for future shipment.
3. The supplier does not produce to stock and requires two or three months or more lead time as a condition of accepting an order from a customer.

In every case the order for future shipment should have a ship date that is far enough in the future that the supplier can reduce inventory required to service the customer's order. If a supplier is paying a customer a discount for orders for shipment only days from now, it seems poor operating strategy to pay the customer any incentive for the order at all.

Orders for future shipment from the supplier's standpoint should serve the purpose of avoiding inventory investment to cover forecast error. With this as a definition of orders for future shipment we can define whether or not to include orders for future shipment in the item's demand history.

Orders for future shipment should be excluded from the item's demand history if they can be produced or procured from the time they are received until the time they must be shipped. Then when the company receives orders for future shipment they should be added to the gross requirements in the resource planning system as a special requirement.

If orders for future shipment must be included in the item's demand history, then the upcoming gross requirement for the item should be the mechanical forecast or the sum of in-house orders for future shipment, whichever is higher. As soon as a company starts following this procedure it eliminates most of the need for the complex consuming the forecast procedure.

One last thing: if orders for future shipment must be part of the item's demand history, they should show in the month they are required to ship.

2. Wholesalers

Wholesalers also make use of orders for future shipment. Wholesalers buy cheap and sell dear. Customers pay wholesalers for stocking inventory from numerous suppliers to reduce freight costs and to reduce lead times. At times wholesalers offer pool orders to their customers. The customers order as much as two and three months into the future for delivery. The wholesaler adds up all of his customer orders from a particular supplier and writes an order on that supplier. When the goods arrive from the supplier the wholesaler breaks bulk and distributes it to his various customers. These orders for future shipment allow the wholesaler to perform the break bulk function without risking inventory investment waiting for uncertain future customer orders. These pool orders or orders for future shipment for the wholesaler should be excluded from the regular demand history for the wholesaler and from the regular forecast of the wholesaler's demand.

In Harrisburg at the Farm Show Building or in Nashville at the Grand Ole Opry, American Hardware would invite in literally thousands of suppliers to display their goods. The thirty-seven hundred customers that American had would walk up and down the aisles where the suppliers had the goods displayed. They would have pre-printed order forms for the goods, and just as though they were shopping in a supermarket they would order six leaf rakes, a dozen hoses, twelve wheelbarrows, three TV sets, all for delivery sometime in the future. American used to boast that they sold a million dollars an hour at one of these markets. I'm sure it's even a larger figure now.

At the end of the market American's computers would add up all of the orders by item, by supplier, and place purchase orders on their suppliers in order to ship the customer's market orders at some future date. None of these orders were included in American Hardware's demand history. The pool orders for the market were in DRP as a special requirement. The customers who purchased this way from American Hardware earned special discounts on the merchandise they purchased and received special dating allowances. American offered these incentives because the company did not have to risk inventory investment to support unknown future customer demand.

3. Retailers

Retailers also make use of orders for future shipment. Many retail stores offer the public the stock they have on display but also have order books where they will order in for a customer and notify the customer when the goods are available. Order-ins are tremendous advantages to the retailer because, once again, the retailer risks no money in inventory investment.

When the customer comes in to pick up the order-in, the customer is in the store and the retailer has the opportunity to show the customer the goods in his store one more time. In other words, the order-ins are traffic builders. Most retailers still charge full price on order-in merchandise. They actually should discount these sales, since they do earn such high return on their limited time investment.

It's fairly obvious that order-ins should not be part of a retailer's demand history for stocking goods in the store.

Orders for future shipment ideally should be excluded from demand history and excluded from forecasted demand. The orders for future shipment that are booked should be added to the gross requirements in a resource planning environment as a special requirement.

Unusual Demand

There are all kinds of exotic formulas for filtering demand errors. They probably filter 90 percent of the demand that actually should have been included in the demand history. Some of the more exotic procedures include calculating the average forecast error, converting that into a probabilistic model, and excluding any demand that falls outside the extremes of the forecast error. This is a great way of reducing forecast error, because if you don't allow any demand that falls outside the range of your expected forecast error your forecasts by definition become more accurate. We're saying this with tongue in cheek. Please don't use this method.

Another simpler method of filtering erroneous demand is to say any demand that's more than 100 percent increase over the last quarter and more than 100 percent increase over the same quarter last year is suspect and someone should look at it. Actually, we dislike that procedure just as much as the more exotic procedure.

The best way to find demand errors is to challenge demand at the customer-item level. When the customer orders five eight-thousand-megawatt gasoline generators the system should kick out that order at the customer level and someone should call the customer and ask them whether or not they really meant to order those five generators. And if they did not mean to order those five generators that demand should be stricken before it's summarized by item.

It's hard for the manufacturer, the wholesaler, and the retailer to get at true demand. Some companies offer customers a prepaid freight if they order a minimum-sized dollar quantity. Customers have been known to take advantage of this by ordering big-ticket items that they know are not in stock in order to make the minimum order requirement. These imaginary orders for big-ticket items inflate demand. Worse yet, some customers order big-ticket items and return them in order to make their minimum freight. Again this inflates demand, and it's even a more costly practice.

Some customers call up to check whether or not some things are in stock. If they're not in stock they don't place the orders. These orders that are never recorded in the booking data understate the demand for items. Retailers have a particular problem getting a handle on true demand. If a customer comes into a retail store and does not find an item he's looking for, he walks out of the store and the retailer may never realize there was a demand for the item at all. The best way for a retailer to avoid understating demand is to be in stock, and the best way for a retailer to make sure he is in stock is this:

In Gadsden, Alabama, I visited a large home center with Robert Cohn, the executive vice president. Robert had shown me a computer listing of his out-of-stocks, and he suggested that he was going to use the computer listing to measure customer service. I suggested to him that it would be much better if we had the department manager count the empty hooks in the store. We went over to the tool section, and Robert, with his pad in hand, recorded the item numbers for the pegs with the empty hooks and the empty bins.

The manager of the tool department watched for a while from a distance and finally couldn't stand it any longer and came over and started following us around. He asked, "Robert, what are you doing?"

Robert said, "Well, Bernie and I are checking out-of-stocks, empty hooks like this one here." Robert pointed to one.

The department manager said, "Oh, Robert, that's not an empty hook. That item has been discontinued, and we haven't taken down the hook yet."

Robert asked, "What about this one?"

The department manager said, "Oh, this merchandise is on the wrong hook, and it should be on that hook."

Robert asked, "What about this one?"

Then the store manager said, "Well, Robert, that's in the back room. We just have to bring the merchandise up and put it on the hook."

Robert asked, "And what about this one?"

The department manager said, "Oh, well, we aren't reordering that one out of the warehouse, Robert; we're waiting to try and build up a big enough order to get a discount."

Robert said, "Oh."

So anyway, Robert and I decided the best way to measure customer service and improve customer service at the retail level was to have the store manager count the number of outs at least every time he ordered. That simple procedure has brought Robert's retail in stock up to the 95 percent level, and at that time he reduced his inventory from $6,000,000 to $4,800,000. The point is, the best way to record demand history at the retail level is to make sure to be in stock.

Shipments

Many companies don't record demand. For their demand history they have shipments. The major problem with shipments as a demand history input to Focus Forecasting is that when a item really gets hot there's a great risk of out-of-stock. If the out-of-stock occurs, the period immediately following the high demand period shows zero. These high-volume periods followed by zero shipments distort Focus Forecasting demand history. Of course at the retail level there's no alternative; the only thing that can be recorded is history of shipments, and the only solution is to be in stock.

But the manufacturer and wholesaler do have alternatives. Customers write electronic orders, customers fill out order forms, and salesmen take orders; these orders should be recorded as demand history. There's no reason for a manufacturer or wholesaler to be using a shipment history to forecast the future. If a company has a shipment history and is about to start up Focus Forecasting, the best thing to do is to run some computer program to fill in those zeros that immediately follow the high shipment month. The second thing to do is switch over to demand history as soon as possible.

Shipments have another major problem. Companies are always working against goals or budgets or profit plans. Companies scramble to make those profit plans at the end of a quarter or at the end of a year. Some companies even hold back on shipments to keep a little bit tucked away for a rainy day. Salesmen, in particular, who receive incentive compensation on making goals are known for tucking away some shipments that can be released when they're in a hole trying to make their goal. The result of these practices distorts the shipment history. Shipments tend to peak at the end of the month, at the end of a quarter, or at the end of the year.

Companies have been guilty of having 366-day shipment years when it's not even leap year. Once a company starts robbing the next period to make goals this period, they get hooked, like drug addicts, and like drug addicts they always need a little more month after month, quarter after quarter, and year after year. When the day of reckoning comes it's compounded by years of borrowing business from the future.

Even without financial chicanery, companies sometimes offer promotions and special-price deals that don't actually add any volume. All they do is move up the shipment of the goods from the supplier to the customer. Some of these incentives create artificial peak loads and overtime in the company. Later on these same incentives cause slump periods and idle capacity and shut down.

When management in a company is measured, something should be done to eliminate these mickey-mouse procedures, because they create more economic waste than the value of any short-term profit increase that can be derived.

Backorders

All companies are out of stock sometimes, or at least they should be. If they are never out of stock they probably have very low return on investment even with high gross profit. Never being out of stock is like having an insurance policy that has no deductible. The inventory-carrying cost premiums are enormous. When retailers are out of stock they sometimes can catch the future business with rain checks, particularly on promoted items. When wholesalers are out of stock, generally speaking, the customer will cancel the original order and order someplace else. Just by definition, a wholesaler is a middleman in distributing merchandise. If the wholesaler doesn't have it available, another wholesaler or supplier will. Manufacturers of brand names are in a situation where if the customer's order can't be shipped there is a possibility of back-ordering the demand for future shipment.

This is the ideal situation for building demand history for input into a Focus Forecasting system. Demand history should be just that, an aggregation by item and time period of a customer's demands on the company. Whether the company ships the item or back-orders the item is of no consequence to the recording of demand history for forecasting the future. Wherever possible, manufacturing companies should back-order customer demand that they cannot ship at once. This creates the most accurate picture of demand history for forecasting.

No Backorders

Wholesalers in particular are faced with a no-backorder situation. When the customer orders, if the customer can't get the goods, generally speaking, the customer cancels his order and orders someplace else. Sometimes the wholesaler deletes the canceled customer's orders from the wholesaler's demand history. Then the wholesaler winds up with a shipment history that, as we mentioned before, is of no real value for forecasting the future. On the other hand, though, if the wholesaler records the customer's demand even after the customer canceled it, the wholesaler runs another risk.

If the customer can't get the goods someplace else, the customer may reorder the goods from the wholesaler week after week. What would have been demand for ten pieces of an item in a month turns into demand of forty pieces of the item for a month. This inflated demand is disastrous to demand history for forecasting the future. The inflated demand must be eliminated. A company's computer can keep track of item cancellations by customer and by quantity. Suppose customer A orders ten pieces of item 12345 and the company is unable to ship those ten pieces. The ten pieces are recorded as demand. Now if next week customer A again orders ten pieces of 12345 that second order is not counted as demand. That inflated demand is eliminated.

If customer A then orders fifteen pieces of item 12345 an additional five more pieces are recorded as demand. After the company ships some 12345 to the customer or after a period of time—one or two months—the company once again starts to record demand for that customer for that item, the assumption being that if the customer had the item he would have used it, consumed it, or resold it in that period of time.

So companies that can't backorder should eliminate inflated demand from their demand history.

Missed Orders

In industries that sell commodity items it is a common practice that a customer will call up to inquire about inventory availability of an item that's in short supply. The customer may call three or four different suppliers and only place the order with the supplier who can deliver at once. At CXA, a part of North American ICI, they make dynamite initiators. They sell these dynamite initiators to distributors around Canada. CXA is one of very few suppliers of dynamite initiators. So if a customer goes to one of CXA's distributors for a particular fuse and they don't have it, the customer may leave that order with that distributor. The customer may order the same fuse from another distributor and maybe even a third. The ultimate customer will only take one delivery of fuses, but the customer's order at the three distributorships is multiplied three times by the time CXA receives the distributors' orders.

Fortunately, CXA has DRP set up with its major distributors so CXA can recognize a duplicate order for future delivery from three different distributors to the same customer.

Most companies do not place demand on their system unless the customer gives them a firm order. Of course the best way to eliminate the problem of missed orders is to have the goods in stock in the first place. Where the goods are not in stock the company receiving the inquiry about the goods' availability should include that demand in the demand history. If the company doesn't include these inquiries in demand history the company probably will never have the goods in stock when the customer calls.

Inflated Demand

Some years ago there was a story about a housewife who was severely injured in Japan while in a panicky stampede to get a roll of toilet paper. Someone had spread the rumor in Japan that there was going to be a shortage of toilet paper. Retailers rushed to super-markets to stock up on toilet paper. Supermarkets and distributors placed rush orders on manufacturers. Eventually the false rumor that there was going to be a shortage of toilet paper happened. Toilet paper can be manufactured relatively quickly. Within a month there was enough toilet paper in Japan to reach from Tokyo to the moon and back.

Back in the 1960s at Warner's World Famous Girdles and Bras one of the hottest features going was stretch-strap bras made from lycra from DuPont. It was all the rage, and people tried to corner the market on stretch-strap material. Every bra house—Bali, Form Fit, Playtex, Warner's, Laros, Cross Your Heart—everybody, placed order after order for stretch straps. As it turned out, in the actual construc-tion of the bra stretch straps were engineeringly unsound. It caused insecurity among the female users and they quickly gave up the stretch strap and in short order there were enough stretch straps to go around the world once or maybe even twice.

In the beginning of spring when my customers at American Hard-ware kept ordering snow shovels and related winter items, chasing the end of season from me, I would write an article in *News from Butler* suggesting that an early spring could create shortages of spring goods. That generally got the customers moving on ordering their spring goods. Nothing inflates demand like shortages; real or unreal doesn't matter, because if it's an unreal shortage eventually it will be real.

Black & Decker tried to get around this problem by keeping track of how much of their inventory was actually out in the world versus consumer demand. That way if unrealistic shortages occurred by people building unreasonable inventories Black & Decker knew that the demand was inflated and eventually it would peter out.

A better solution, though, is resource planning from your major customers. Resource planning would show whether your major customer was building inventory or actually was experiencing major sell-throughs.

Interbranch Demand

There are more companies forecasting what their own distribution centers will buy from them than there are companies forecasting ultimate customer demand. Most companies make the error of forecasting global customer demand and expecting the orders from their distribution centers to add up to that global customer demand. Some companies actually try to forecast the orders that their distribution centers will place on their consolidation center or manufacturing center.

World Wide Trading in Hayward, California, imports from all around the world into a consolidation center. They forecast what their five major distribution centers around the United States will order from the Hayward Consolidation Center. Their longer-term scenario is to forecast at the distribution-center level by item. They will use DRP at the distribution-center level to develop a schedule of planned orders against the Hayward Consolidation Center. Then by supplier they'll use DRP at the consolidation-center level to import from overseas and to break bulk to the individual distribution centers. This makes a lot more sense than forecasting what your own distribution centers will be buying from you in the future.

Random Promotion Demand

In St. Louis we tried to use Focus Forecasting for Rexall Drug Company. As a first order of business we started to look at their demand data to see what sorts of strategies would forecast Rexall product demand. After checking four or five items it became obvious that nothing could forecast Rexall product demand. For no reason at all sales would suddenly die for one or two months and then take off unexpectedly three and four times the normal demand.

In this crazy world people always delight in confounding the experts. They said, "See, we're special; Focus Forecasting won't work on our products."

We said, "We agree. We don't understand what's the matter with the way your demand behaves. The way your demand behaves, it almost looks as though you had random promotion offerings of a product."

"We do," they said. "We can pick a product anytime and run a promotion on it. That's what fouls up the demand so much."

There is no system in the world that is going to forecast accurately if you have random promotion demand in your history. There are only two ways to handle random promotion demand. One is when you offer the item under the special promotion, offer it with a separate stock-keeping unit number. Prefix it with a "P" or something. Capture the off-price sales when people order with this special stock-keeping unit number. When you have an upcoming promotion, forecast that promotion as a special requirement on your resource planning system. You can't use Focus Forecasting based on history of any sort to forecast upcoming promotion demand.

There are systems for forecasting promotion demand, and they're in appendix 2 of *Focus Forecasting: Computer Techniques for Inventory Control.*

Keep random promotion demand out of the item's demand history.

If the item's demand history must include random promotion demand history, before the demand is recorded in history it should be reduced by a factor reflecting that the item was being promoted. This is the only other way to keep random promotion demand from destroying any chance at future forecast accuracy.

If your customers are randomly promoting your product to their customers, there's no need to capture that demand as separate demand. It's only when your company is distorting the normal demand pattern by offering promotions at a special price that the demand must be captured separately. If you regularly promote an item at the same time of the year, year in and year out, there's no need to keep the promotion demand separate.

Forecast without random promotion demand in the history. Add forecasts of upcoming random promotions as special requirements in DRP.

Redoing the Order Entry System

In 1960 at graduate school I did a survey of thirty of the Fortune 500 companies to find out what their MIS (Management Information Systems) departments were doing. The number-one priority was redoing the order entry system. Nothing has changed.

In all of the companies that we have had the opportunity to visit in different parts of the world we find that the single highest priority project, ongoing and everlasting, is redoing the order entry. MIS is always redoing the order entry. Why is that?

1. When you think about MIS, they have a product and their everyday production work is processing the orders and running the invoices. That's usually part of their data-processing function. Since it's their own function, they can always find ways of making what they do more effective and they're always rewriting the programs to get rid of inefficient procedures to make the order entry better. They can do this without any input from any other line department . . . it's a wonderful thing.
2. There are always new computers coming down the pike, computers that give more data-processing power for the dollar. Since there are new computers that give more data-processing power for the dollar, MIS needs little incentive to start reprogramming the applications or redesigning the data bases for this new megacomputer complex.
3. Right up there with redoing the order entry is building a data base for the company. Building a data base for the company is analogous to writing a book with all of the answers in it for any question that anyone will ever ask. It is, of course, a Don Quixote exercise that will never come to fruition but it keeps data-processing people busy forever, with little or no payback. It's a favorite of scorekeepers. While redoing the company's data base, redoing the order entry is a natural to provide the information to the data base on orders and sales and shipments and freight costs and what have you. So the third biggest reason for redoing the order entry is to build the company's data base.
4. The company is alive; it's like a living person, always changing, and growing. Companies are always adding new divisions, new products, changing pricing, changing the way they offer freight.

83

The order entry is always out-of-date. It's out-of-date the day it was installed because it's trying to adapt to a company that is always changing.

5. Redoing the order entry is the least-risk application with which any MIS group can get involved. How do you fail at redoing the order entry? Only when the invoices don't come out anymore, and in short order you're able to fix that.

6. The scorekeepers in the company always want more analysis of performance: sales reports, marketing reports, inventory reports, things to nail the manufacturing vice president, the operations vice president, the logistics vice president, the distribution center vice president to the wall. The order entry is the base of information that's best available to present that data.

Companies spend literally millions of dollars on keeping score on how well the company is performing. Those same companies sometimes won't spend thousands of dollars to give their people the tools to actually perform better in the first place. Usually if the MIS group is involved in redoing the order entry, they're doing performance analyses at the same time.

So if you want to clean up your demand data and your MIS group tells you to wait until they finish redoing the order entry, remind them that the number-one job of a company is improving customer service and most customers rate customer service on how well the company ships, not on how pretty the invoice looks or on how well we tell them when we'll ship the goods we were supposed to have in stock in the first place.

Remember, too, that redoing the order entry and building the company data base are two tasks that have not been completed in the past thirty years and won't be completed in the next thirty years. Finally, keep in mind that scorekeeping is only a number-two priority. Improved performance is number-one. Remember to keep the dog wagging the tail.

The Ideal Order Entry System

The ideal order entry system should be purchased from some company that does order entry systems for a living. If somebody has to redo the order entry, let it be a professional at redoing ordering entries. It means we must make some great sacrifices in the color of our invoice stock and in how the columns are lined up. But think of the trade-off—it means that we will be able to use our MIS group for some high payoff areas while our competition is redoing their order entry systems.

To that outside company we say: GIVE US REAL DEMAND HISTORY.

1. Give us a demand history that is what our customer ordered free of inflated demands.
2. Give us a demand history that captures random promotion data and orders for future shipment as separate demand category items.
3. Don't just add the interbranch demands in with the regular customer demands.
4. Allow a way of finding order entry inaccuracies at the customer-item level.
5. Allow procedures for companies to add products and change pricing strategies and change freight and add divisions without reinvesting major development dollars.
6. Come up with standards for electronic data interchange so that companies not only send orders but projections of future planned orders as well.
7. Provide a user data base based on your experience.
8. Give the user some kind of information retrieval language to do his sales analysis and marketing analysis tailored to his own company.
9. Include some measures of customer service for the total company for the product category for the distribution center.
10. Don't get involved in resource planning or in forecasting. Be an expert in order entry.

This chapter tried to give you some insight into creating sound demand history for your company. Without a simultaneous effort in creating a sound demand history it's a waste of time to install a new forecasting system in most companies. Next are some special forecast considerations.

Chapter Ten

Special Forecast Considerations

Promotion Items

If you take as a definition of selling "communicating the value of a product to a potential customer," it becomes obvious why marketing pushes for more and more promotions. If a product is a value at ten dollars it's even of more value at nine dollars. If the price gets low enough, it's no sales effort at all to sell it to the customer. So sales and marketing departments that don't have any profit responsibility continually push for lower-priced promoted products. And there are tough customers out there. They want the best price every time; they want a better price than anybody else even if it's illegal. They put tremendous pressure on competitive suppliers to reduce their every-day prices. They know how to negotiate.

"Is this item ever on sale? If it is, I want the sale price now."
"You offer dating on this product, can we have a discount instead?"
"Don't you fellows ever have any excess inventory you want to get rid of?"

There are tremendous pressures on the salesman to sell his products at less than regular price. Government commissions found toilet bowls that cost five hundred dollars apiece. After their study the purchasing agents in the government really became price-conscious. But what a travesty; people don't understand the interchangeability of price and volume. As soon as the purchasing agents became more price-conscious they started buying truckloads and carloads of things they wouldn't need for months into the future in order to secure the best price.

Promotions lose value when they cause consumers to stock up on products just because of the special price. It's like the story about the man who was offered an Indian elephant. He said, "No way. Why in heaven would I ever want an Indian elephant? What would I do with an Indian elephant? Where would I put him?"

The salesperson said, "But the Indian elephant only costs one thousand dollars."

The man said, "That sounds very good, but really, what would I do with an Indian elephant? What would I feed him? How would I wash him?"

The salesperson said, "I'll tell you what; I'll give you two Indian elephants for one thousand dollars," and the man said, "Sold."

All over the United States, retailers and wholesalers and manufacturers are stocking up on inventories that they won't be using in the distant future and perhaps will never use for the simple reason that they can buy it at a promotion price.

There are really just two kinds of promotions. There are promotions that move goods from the supplier to the immediate customer. What these promotions do is preempt the competition. They flood the customer's shelves with the promoted inventory so there's no room for the competitor's inventory. They really don't add anything of value; they just move demand from one brand to another.

The second type of promotion not only sells goods to the immediate customer, but sells goods to the consumer as well. This is where the promotion includes national advertising, direct mail, or telephone selling. In those cases there is an actual value added. The consumer is made aware of the value of the product and actually consumes more of the product.

How do you forecast these separate promotion demands? The best way to forecast these separate promotion demands is to treat them as goals rather than as forecasts. If a merchant adds an item to a direct-mail piece, the merchant should estimate what dollar volume of that item will sell as a result. If a salesman is responsible for selling a promotion to his major customers, he should have an overall dollar volume responsibility for that promotion. These dollar value figures on promotions can be converted into individual item sales. Once the individual item sales forecasts have been calculated they can be added to the gross requirements of the company as special requirements.

One-shot Promotions

There are a lot of one-shot promotions. For example, companies sometimes have a Twenty-fifth Anniversary Sale or a Fiftieth Anniversary Sale. As part of that sale they may select items and offer them at a special promotion price. They may send out a great number of direct-mail pieces. They may use radio and TV and national advertising to generate volume for the products.

The best way to forecast a one-shot promotion is to forecast a time period in terms of sales that the company would normally expect to sell. If this is a once-in-a-lifetime offering, for example, the company may forecast that it is going to sell a year's supply of the product at the normal rate of sales. If the worse case happens, the most the company will have to carry is a twelve months' supply.

Ideally, if the company can pick products that it is overstocked with as the one-time offer, then the forecasting is not nearly as important. Sometimes one-shot promotions become an allocation rather than a forecast. When one company decided to run 3-D glasses for the halftime show at Super Bowl XXIII, they allocated so many 3-D glasses to each of their distributors throughout the world. There was no forecasting involved. The forecast was the allotment.

One-shot promotions can cause an awful lot of enemies when a company runs short. The best strategy in forecasting one-shot promotions is to forecast on the high side and have prepared a method of discounting and dumping the excess created. Part of any strategy for one-shot promotions should limit the number of stock-keeping units offered in the promotion. The odds of getting burned with serious overstock or serious shortage of a one-shot promotion goes up exponentially as stock-keeping units are added. In other words, a company runs a fifty-fifty chance of an overstock or understock if it offers one item; if it offers two items it has a fifty-fifty chance of both an overstock and an understock; etc.

So on one-shot promotions it's best to put all your eggs in one basket and watch it. Set up supply lines so that the company can fill in very quickly. Set up channels for dumping excesses before the advertising material runs its course.

Cyclical Promotions

Then there are the cyclical promotions . . . the Father's Day, Mother's Day, Spring, Summer, Fall, Gift, Valentine's Day, Super Bowl promotions that go on year after year. These promotions are a constant source of agony for most suppliers. The most significant impact on cyclical promotion demand is advertising impact.

Take circular advertising for example. An item featured on the cover page of the circular advertising has twice the advertising impact of anything spread throughout the pages of the circular. Not only that, but it's wise to forecast a little high on the cover page anyway. If a customer comes into the store and the store is out of the item featured on the cover page there's hell to pay. Items featured on the back page and in the center of the circular also have heavy advertising impact. Items that are featured in the circular and reinforced with television or radio advertising receive even greater advertising impact.

Then there's the question of value. An item has a normal selling price. If it's promoted at a special price, that increases the value of that item to the consumer. The seasonal aspect of the item can add to its advertising impact. If it's a heart-shaped cake pan during the Valentine holiday, that's worth almost as much as the cover page. If it's a snow shovel during a blizzard, that's worth as much as two cover pages.

When merchants are placing items in a circular they should bid sales dollars for the space taken up in the circular. They should be held accountable for generating those sales dollars. Their forecasts of how much product they will sell in the circular should be added to the regular gross requirements in the company as special requirements.

January Specials

Some companies produce specials just for promotions. For instance, in the white goods industry they produce what they call January specials. Sometimes the January special is the same stock-keeping unit. It's just the stock-keeping unit number prefixed with an S for special. Usually at the same time that the special is nationally offered to the retailer a newspaper ad or direct mail flyer is sent to the ultimate consumer. In all of the advertising and the sales at the retail level, the wholesale level, and the manufacturing level, the promoted stock-keeping unit should be identified separately from the regular item. Sales of the special promotion item can relieve a single inventory that's maintained for both the promotion and for regular sales; that's not the problem. It's just that we don't want the demand history impacted by surges that are artificially caused by the company's special pricing, special advertising, and special marketing efforts.

It's much better to treat promotions as special requirements on the company's inventory. We'll get into the details of how to add special requirements as a separate part of company forecasts in part III.

Seasonal Items

Focus Forecasting requires at least twenty-four months of demand history to analyze an item to see if it is indeed seasonal. Take, for example, trying to forecast Christmas trees. If Focus Forecasting used "whatever we sold in the last three months will probably sell in the next three months" we would have a disaster for forecasting Christmas trees.

On seasonal items Focus Forecasting must choose formulas that are related to last year. The best formulas for Christmas trees are:

1. We'll probably sell as many Christmas trees as last year.
2. We'll probably have the average company increase.

Focus Forecasting doesn't require anyone to tell it that this specific item is a seasonal item. It works, based on looking at the formulas that worked in the recent past. For seasonal items it automatically locks in on and focuses on seasonal approaches.

A caution here: Don't try to put in seasonal curves from similar items to forecast new items. New items go through a pipeline filling cycle that totally distorts normal seasonality. For more on that see

Focus Forecasting: Computer Techniques for Inventory Control, pp. 23–25.

Lumpy Demand Items

Most forecasting systems are statistical techniques. In other words, they depend on normal distributions and other probabilistic phenomena occurring in a company's demand history. Focus Forecasting is not a statistical technique, rather, it substitutes simulation for expected statistical outcomes.

Pereto's Law says 80 percent of the volume occurs in 20 percent of the items. That says 80 percent of our items display lumpy demand—80 percent of our items are not statistically reliable. A while back at the World's Fair in Long Island at Flushing Meadows, there was a booth that IBM had set up where they dropped a great volume of black rubber balls down a chute. These rubber balls would hit pins at random, and as they fell down they would form a normal distribution. Time after time the balls would drop down the chute and be scooped up again and let loose, and each time, after enough balls had fallen, they would form that normal distribution. Yes, by the laws of large numbers as those balls fell down randomly they normally distributed.

What if IBM had only dropped twenty balls or thirty balls? Ah, there goes the normal distribution. Normal distribution depends on large numbers. Normal distribution says that if you go out one standard deviation from the mean you will cover 84 percent of all occurrences. If you go out two standard deviations you'll cover 97 percent of all occurrences, and if you go out three standard deviations you'll cover 99.7 percent of all occurrences. If you look at those normal distributions, those beautiful bell-shaped curves, under a magnifying glass, though, if you look at the tail of those normal distributions, you'll find that they're not normally distributed. The reason is there is not sufficient data in the tail of a normal distribution to behave with statistical reliability. There are whole sciences devoted to studying these distributions. They are called Statistics of Extremes.

So 80 percent of the items in a company generate less than

20 percent of the company's volume. These items have very sparse demand. They are not normally distributed. Statistical techniques run into all kinds of problems when they forecast these items. In other words, statistical techniques run into all kinds of problems on 80 percent of a company's items.

Even on some of the high-volume items, statistical techniques have problems when those high-volume items are out of season. Take flyswatters for example. In January, February, and March in northern latitudes very few flyswatters are sold, maybe ten in January, five in February, and ten in March. When you use the statistical forecasting technique, which all other forecasting approaches, other than Focus Forecasting, are, they look at these low-volume periods and draw totally absurd conclusions. For instance, if there was a 100 percent increase in fly swatter demand in January, February, and March statistical concepts would probably forecast 50 to 100 percent increases in sales in July, August, and September. Of course, percentage increases of flyswatters in January, February, and March have nothing whatsoever to do with flyswatter sales in June, July, and August.

Flyswatter Forecast Problem
Traditional Approach

	x7		x8		x9	
	Sales History	% of Year	Sales History	% of Year	Sales History	% of Year
1st Qtr	30	.15	20	.08	80	.115
2nd Qtr	1010	5.05	200	.80		2.925
3rd Qtr	18000	90.00	23880	95.52		92.760
4th Qtr	960	4.80	900	3.60		4.200
Total	20000	100.00	25000	100.00		100.000

In this example traditional approaches would forecast outrageously high in-season flyswatter sales. Focus Forecasting would forecast the same quantity as last year.

92

Focus Forecasting can forecast lumpy demand items as well as any person or system in the world. It chooses the formula that works the best in the recent past for the lumpy item and uses that formula to project the future. In the example of flyswatters it would probably choose "we'll probably sell what we sold last year" or "we'll probably have the average warehouse increase over last year."

Sometimes the past demand will show a very erratic behavior over the course of a year. This is particularly true on lumpy demand, low-volume items. When Focus Forecasting evaluates these lumpy patterns and selects a formula, it may well select an average as a projection of the future. When Focus Forecasting displays this average next to past years' demand it shows basically a straight line versus sporadic demand patterns over the past three or four years. This makes some people uncomfortable, since they know that the demand won't occur in a straight line month after month.

These people have a tendency to want to introduce some false seasonality into the Focus Forecasting projection. That makes the data look like the forecast is more reasonable. Of course it's not. There's no more reason on sporadic demand items to expect any kind of a seasonality than to expect a straight line. The straight month average forecast is the best guess of what each month going out into the future will be. If the demand data exhibited seasonality, Focus Forecasting would have selected seasonal formulas and projected seasonality going out into the future in the first place.

We had a client who was "correcting Focus Forecasting." It seemed on some low-volume items where the client expected seasonality it was forecasting zero future volume. The client had a problem with accepting a zero forecast. The client changed the zero forecasts to more tasteful seasonal projections of future volume. Unfortunately, by taking thousands of low-volume demand items where the system was forecasting zero or practically zero future demand and putting in demand to represent some kind of seasonal pattern, the client ensured the company major inventory excesses in the future.

If last year avocado wall clock demand was 1-0-0-8-1 and this year Focus Forecasting is forecasting 1-0-0-8-1, that probably is the best forecast of the future. For this sporadic lumpy low-volume demand item there is not reason in the world to smooth out the forecast so that it comes out to 2-2-2-2-2 or to eliminate the 8 or undertake any other purely argumentative procedure. Indeed, whenever anyone

93

arbitrarily makes changes to Focus Forecasting of this type they should very carefully measure whether it has improved the forecasting or made it worse for future months. We hear, "Oh, what difference does it make? This is a low-volume item that doesn't amount to a hill of beans." Well, although low-volume items account for only 20 percent of the sales, in many companies they account for 80 percent of the inventory excesses. Remember, there are four times as many low-volume items as high-volume items.

Lumpy demand items are difficult to forecast accurately. Some are so random that the recent past is not an indicator of the future. Then the best procedure to use for forecasting is a simple three-month average of the past history. It also is the best procedure for forecasting the last three digits in a telephone number on a page in the directory. If a three-month average is the best formula, Focus Forecasting will select it.

Don't make the mistake of assuming a person can forecast lumpy demand items more accurately than Focus Forecasting. Play "Can You Outguess Focus Forecasting?" first to decide if you really can.

Discontinued Items

When an item is discontinued there's a strong temptation to take the demand history from the discontinued item and plug it into the replacement item. If the fact that the new item replacing the old item is unknown to the customer then it's all right to take the old demand history and put it into the new item. But if we are actually telling the customer that we are discontinuing the old item and here is the new item that you should start ordering, then it's better to let Focus Forecasting pick strategies based on what's actually happening. Let the system continue to forecast the demand on the discontinued item until the demand ceases. Let Focus Forecasting forecast the demand on the new item as the new item demand gradually builds month by month.

In Joe Orlicky's book, *MRP Material Requirements Planning,* there is a detailed explanation of supersession logic for new items replacing old items.

Dependent Demand Items

Sometimes Focus Forecasting is not the answer. Where a company's sales depend on the ordering of a small number of very large customers it doesn't make any sense to forecast those customers' demands. In that situation it makes much more sense to use DRP.

While I was at American Hardware, we chose Black & Decker as the first supplier for our DRP system. We used Focus Forecasting to forecast our sales and to feed gross requirements to DRP. But in addition to the system input we added in our estimates of what we would be selling in Father's Day promotions and gift promotions and spring promotions and pool sales and special discount offerings. The total gross requirements in my company were netted against the current available inventory using DRP, and what we gave Black & Decker was our planned orders for the future.

Black & Decker started to use our planned orders, treating their gross requirements as dependent on our planned order schedules, rather than forecasting our demand as though it were an independent variable. The result over a period of time was that Black & Decker service to our customers through our warehouses exceeded the average customer service that we gave across the board to our customers after a period of just months. In the process we earned additional discounts from Black & Decker and improved our inventory turnover.

There are only two systems that I know of that will outforecast Focus Forecasting. One of them is DRP for dependent demand items. The other is consensus.

Longer-term Forecasts

By far the most common forecasting time periods in business are months. Most commonly sales history and demand histories are saved in monthly buckets. Focus Forecasting can forecast one month, six months, one year, or one and a half years, but generally it forecasts in monthly intervals. If the forecast formula that was chosen was that we'd probably have the average company increase, then the system would create monthly forecasts month by month out into the future a month, six months, a year, a year and a half. By multiplying last year's monthly sales history by the average company increase, each month would have a unique forecast. This is particularly significant on items that display seasonal patterns year after year, like snow shovels, Valentine's day cards, Christmas tree lights, and Super Bowl hats. If the formula "we'll probably sell whatever we sold the last three months" were chosen, then the system would calculate a monthly average and extrapolate that monthly average out a month, six months, a year, a year and a half, whatever was required. If that formula were chosen, every month would look like every other month for the next year and a half.

Another method for forecasting further into the future is to pretend that after each quarter Focus Forecasting has forecasted, that quarter is now part of the history for forecasting the next quarter.

Monthly buckets haven't just been chosen by accident. Monthly groupings of demand history take out some of the noise that would be present if daily or weekly sales history buckets were used. Of course, there are some industries where the volumes are so large that it would be worthwhile to keep daily or weekly buckets. This is particularly true in the food industry and in commodity industries. A truckload of cigarettes is worth over a million dollars. Certainly it's worth the effort to keep a daily sales history on cigarettes.

Once the forecast is created in monthly buckets, it can be converted into weekly intervals or even daily intervals. In this area we've observed some consultants get overzealous in trying to get the exact breakdown of the monthly forecast into daily and weekly increments. They get into the number of work days in a month, what holidays occur, whether or not it's a leap year, and all such minutia. Since forecast errors average at least in the 20 percent range, it's not worth getting into this much detail in trying to break the gross requirements into daily buckets. It is worthwhile breaking the monthly forecast into as realistic picture of weekly demand as possible.

Some industries follow the absurd practice of shipping the bulk of their goods at the end of the month. This is another part of the shoot-yourself-in-the-foot cycle where we manage to keep the bulk of the company idle the first three weeks of the month and then work overtime the last week of the month in a frantic, chaotic panic. If this is what you do, our initial advise to you would be to stop doing it. If you must do it, then when you convert monthly system output to weekly increments, weight the last week of the month more heavily. There are always our accounting friends who love 4-4-5 and 4-5-4 and four Fridays in a month and in striving for consistency they create their own calendars. If that's the way the months are defined in the history there won't be any problem—Focus Forecasting will forecast those 4-4-5 months as they occur. Then of course there are always the thirteen-month advocates. They find that 13 divides into 52 much better than 12, and therefore they have four weeks in every month. Again, if that's the monthly input to Focus Forecasting there shouldn't be any problem. Seasonality should still be displayed properly.

In our opinion, if thirteen-month years were adopted by business around the world there would be less forecast error and better inventory management as a result. Just the fact of thirteen reviews in a year rather than twelve reviews in a year would improve performance. Of course, companies would trade more work for that improved performance.

If a company is very concerned about longer-term forecasts there is some question as to how the Focus Forecasting formula should be selected. Perhaps formulas shouldn't be selected based on what provided the best quarterly forecast over the last year. Perhaps the method should be selected on what provided the best forecast over the decision period, whatever it was. At this stage in our research we don't really know whether using the recent past outweighs using the relevant time period for the selection of the formula. Simulation in your company should provide the best answer.

Management Overrides

With all the talk about delegating authority and participative management, the real test comes when top management is under pressure. I remember in 1973 during the energy crisis the sales of locking gas caps went from twenty a month to four hundred a week. The buyers, of course, at that time were fixing Focus Forecasting to correct the erroneous demand that was creating erroneous forecasts of how many we would sell in the future. They continually reduced and canceled the proposed purchases that the system was making. The world supply of locking gas caps quickly ran out. Our customers went into a panic, screaming, "How could anyone run out of anything as basic as a locking gas cap?" The president of the company finally got into the act and said, "I can understand us being out of

97

locking gas caps. But I can't understand us not having locking gas caps on order. No matter what, I never want to have to tell any one of our customers that we don't have locking gas caps on order."

I went to the buyers and told them the same thing. "Look, I can understand our suppliers not having locking gas caps, but I never want to have to tell our customers that we don't have any on order."

Up until then the buyers had been canceling the system's suggested purchase orders. About the time the president got involved, the energy crisis started to let up. Focus Forecasting started to project lower locking gas cap sales. Of course the buyers, remembering what I had said, and I, remembering what the president had said, continued to increase the purchase orders. By the end of the energy crisis we had enough locking gas caps to supply the world for the next ten years. I think you still can buy some cheap. I'll give you a number if you are interested.

Locking gas caps were only one example. While locking gas caps were going from twenty a month to four hundred a week, siphon hoses went from twenty a month to four thousand a week. The point is that by the time management is ready to do an override, it's probably just about the right time to move in the opposite direction. It's better to let the forecasting system do its thing and then critique the forecasting system than muddy the waters by overriding the forecast up and down as an everyday matter.

It is much better to work on improving your forecasting system than to work on changing individual forecasts. If a company must change a forecast, it should document the reasons why the forecast was changed. Make sure to measure in the future whether the changed forecast was an improvement or made the forecast worse. In the absence of additional data, our position would be that forecast changes almost always in aggregate make things worse. In other words, in the absence of some hard data that the system doesn't have don't change the forecast.

With a policy of not changing the forecast a company knows that the forecasting system has a certain degree of accuracy that it can depend on year after year. If people constantly change the answers that the forecasting system comes up with, the company doesn't know whether in a period when the forecast was very accurate it was the system or it was the overrides that made it accurate. Delegate the forecasting to the forecasting system; measure its performance, but don't second-guess it.

Either use the forecasting system or get a new forecasting system.

Rules of Thumb

With the complexity of business over the years, management learns to use rules of thumb. Whenever there is insufficient data to prove whether things are true, they fall back on rules of thumb. Here are two examples of this:

1. There was a certain buyer cutting back the purchases on steel garbage cans, the corrugated kind, from Wheeling Corrugated. The forecasts looked reasonable. The purchases didn't seem out of line. Why was he cutting back the purchases? He said, "Well, as a rule of thumb when we offer a promotional garbage can the sales of these regular garbage cans go to hell." With a little research we checked out the sales of the promotional garbage can and the sales of the regular garbage can. As far as we could see, whenever the promotional garbage can was offered the regular garbage can sales went up. I went back to the buyer and bet him twenty-five cents that he would run out of the regular garbage cans. He did! That was a rule of thumb that was totally a disservice.

2. Here's another one. We noticed a buyer cutting back the purchases of hunting license holders. Admittedly, it was after hunting season. He explained, "As a rule of thumb we don't sell too many hunting licenses out of season." We looked at demand history and there was a demand right after the regular hunting season, but we agreed with the buyer and we reduced the purchase and actually corrected the demand history. The following year the same item came up again and we remembered having talked to the buyer. I said, "Hey, this time let's buy what it said." When the orders came in from our customers for the hunting license holder after the normal hunting season, we called them up. They were customers in Vermont and New Hampshire, and we asked them why they were buying hunting license holders after hunting season was over. They explained simply that the ski clubs liked

to use the hunting license holders as name identifiers. Another rule of thumb shot down.

Any time that you are going to change one of the forecasts be very wary of rules of thumb. They can create more problems than they correct.

In the companies that use Focus Forecasting and in companies that use other forecasting systems the major objection we have to what they are doing is that they have people changing forecasts without measuring the impact of these changes. Nine out of ten times people can tell you why a certain forecast of the future will be wrong for all sorts of reasons. "Ah, this is a seasonal product." "Ah, this has lumpy demand; that will never happen again." "Oh, we had a hurricane last year." "Ah, that was a special event, we added a new chain."

We don't trust these rule-of-thumb prognosticators. These are the same sort of things that you see in the local grocery store with the fellows sitting around on the wooden stools making all sorts of uninformed forecasts. It's only of value if somebody measures those forecast changes to see, hey, are we making things more right than wrong? Somewhere along the line we must aggregate all of the changes and see whether the aggregate change in total made things better or worse. If you're using a Focus Forecasting system, almost invariably the unmeasured changes that the company is making to the forecast are not improving the overall forecast accuracy.

Forecasting in Bad Times

I became the inventory manager at American Hardware in February of 1972. Right after I started, I learned that the past three inventory managers had only lasted two years each and they hadn't gone on to noble careers afterward either. One became a controller of a museum out in Arizona; he didn't want to see things changing anymore. Another became a chiropractor; he wanted to work with his hands instead of a computer for a change. And the third one became a watchman on a dam in Chicora, Pennsylvania. I started in February of 1972. We installed Focus Forecasting in December of 1972. The very next year, 1973, the Arabs cut off oil supplies to the United

States and the United States underwent the worst shortage economy in its history.

If in '72 I had installed a more complex system than Focus Forecasting it would have been thrown out. Why? In 1973 the service level to our customers was in the sixties. It was in the sixties because we could not get product from our regular suppliers. All of the buyers were under pressure. The computer systems were under pressure. The inventory management was under pressure. It looked as though I wouldn't last the traditional two years, but one of the beauties was when I walked into the boardroom I could explain how Focus Forecasting worked and everybody understood it. And they thought, *Hum, that's a reasonable approach.* Think to yourself what would have happened if I had to explain exponential smoothing in a board meeting or Box-Jenkins or Cogs or React or some system that used sines and cosines. Not only would the system have disappeared, I might have disappeared right along with it.

Focus Forecasting is the system to have during times of shortage economies and during times of recession or depression. It's easy to explain how it works. That is one of the major advantages of Focus Forecasting over the more complicated approaches.

Need for a Consistent Bias

Let's face it. If you had a forecast that was always 10 percent low you'd think you died and went to heaven. If it were always 10 percent low you could compensate for it with a safety stock. The same is true if you had a forecast that was always 10 percent high. You could compensate for it with lower safety stock.

Over the years, Focus Forecasting does display a consistent bias. A company using this forecasting tool can develop inventory strategies that compensate for this bias. If, however, a company is always changing the future, it will destroy this consistent bias. Once the consistency is destroyed, the company never knows whether the forecast will be high or low and loses the ability to plan an inventory strategy to account for the bias.

A company is fortunate if it has not changed the output from the forecasting system over a period of years. It winds up with a tool that it can depend on for consistent reliability.

We first installed Focus Forecasting in December of 1972. Yet we did not change the Focus Forecasting output in the difficult years of an energy crisis and subsequent recession. We learned how much we could rely on Focus Forecasting in times of extreme increasing sales demand and in times of quickly fading demand. We learned the importance of having a system we could trust for consistency. Focus Forecasting is still hard at work at American Hardware (now known as Servistar®).

Forecasting New Items

Some companies don't really offer a stable product. They have entire line changes from year to year. This is particularly true in fashion businesses like lingerie or furs. Lingerie offerings can include daywear and sleepwear, pajamas, baby dolls, stockings, negligees, panties, and silk and satin accessories. People in this high-fashion business have a real problem when they come out with a new line offering with the various colors and prints. How much should they produce? They want to promote the new offering; where should they put the advertising dollars?

Generally speaking, if they ask the salesman's or the customer's help in forecasting volume over the new line offering, the customer and the salesman cannot relate to total company volumes. Generally speaking, both the salesman and the customer overestimate the worst-selling item volume in the line and underestimate the best-selling volume in the line. No one would dare estimate that the first 5 percent of the items will generate 40 percent of the volume, which is normally the case.

E. I. DuPont saw this problem early in the 1960s. They supplied fibers to the fabric manufacturers. The success of the garment distributors in large measure was the success of the fabric producers. DuPont invented the ranking system. They had a customer from a major retail outlet like Lord & Taylor take the new line offering and rank it from the best-selling item to the worst item. They'd actually have racks set up and have the buyer from Lord & Taylor move the garments around on the rack until they showed the best-seller to worst-seller. Then, rather than ask the customer what quantities they expected to be sold, DuPont just used a ranking curve that was derived from previous

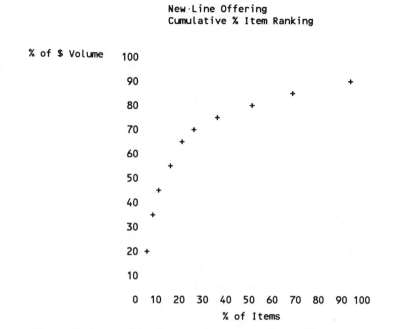

New·Line Offering
Cumulative % Item Ranking

% of $ Volume

% of Items

new-line offerings. If in the previous new-line offerings the number-one selling item generated 8 percent of the volume, then based on the customer's ranking of the number-one item and based on the overall estimate of how much the promotion would sell the volume for that individual item could be estimated.

Unfortunately, even after using this ranking procedure the people who produced the garments were still not brave enough to invest the resources necessary in the best-selling items or leave the worst-selling items as unsupported as they should be. Here is a graphical representation of the ranking system.

Over the years a company can develop a panel of effective rankers. In the beginning the people who dominate the ranking are the company president and the design and engineering departments. In the longer haul, though, the ranking panel should be composed of people who are most accurate in ranking.

When I was director of information systems for Warner's World Famous Girdles & Bras, I reported directly to the president and I had the company's two computers and their department of seventy-five people under my control. I was a young man and wanted to know what my potential was in this apparel company, and I asked my boss, Phil Lamoureux, whether or not I had a shot at becoming the president of one off the divisions. He said to me, "Bernie, being the president of an apparel company isn't necessarily a question of knowledge; it's a question of taste." I took insult at this, wearing my pink button-down shirt and yellow striped tie. I didn't see anything wrong with my taste. Seeing my downcast look, Phil corrected himself quickly and said, "It's not just the question of having good taste; it's a question of having a taste that agrees with the marketplace."

Well, we have to agree with Phil that producing in accordance with the taste in the marketplace is very important. But we're not as convinced that the president is the person who must have that taste. A carefully measured panel using the DuPont ranking system can give excellent taste input to a forecaster of one-time line offerings. And in a fashion business, the company that forecasts the new-line offerings most efficiently wins. They survive; they grow; they take over market share. No other single element in that type of company is more important.

Consensus as a Forecast Tool

There is one forecasting system that is more accurate than Focus Forecasting. We learned about it as part of personal interactive skill development rather than at any statistical or mathematical conference.

The AMA offered a course in group sensitivity. As part of that course, each individual in a group was given a rather complicated treatise on life characteristics of the tsetse fly, a dull subject, believe me. Individually we took a test on the material that we had read. The highest individual score on that test was 84 percent. Without rereading the material, we met as a group and discussed each question on the test, the process being not that majority ruled—in other words, even if nine out of ten voted for an answer, that was not necessarily the answer chosen. The process was that everyone in the group had to agree that it might be the answer. If there was one strong minority objection, that voice had to be brought into agreement before reviewing the next question. The group working the test on the same material without rereading it scored 98 percent accurate. The other two points were not in error. The group was not accustomed to working as a group and did not get to that question in the time allotted for the exercise.

Consensus is an excellent forecasting technique. If all of the people in the company could agree on the volume that would be sold on a new-line offering as a consensus, that would outdo the ranking system or any other approach to new-line offerings. Consensus is the most accurate forecasting system in the world; unfortunately, it's also the most expensive, since it's the process whereby everyone in the group must say that they agree that the solution arrived at could be the correct solution.

Here is another experiment involving consensus. We were given a list of forty-eight items that were left over in a desert after an air crash. The job of our team, all ten of us, was to rank the things we would carry away from the scene in the order that we would need them the most for survival. We had a mixed group of people from all walks of life, some educated, some not, men and women, old and young. One individual in the group would not give up a .45 magnum revolver. We explained to him that the gun in a desert would be of little use for killing snakes or food. We explained that in the desert we would not need the revolver for purposes of defense. But he insisted that the gun would be of value. He couldn't express exactly why, but he felt that the gun would be of value. As the time marched on and we were pressured to go on to the next item on the list, we moved the gun up in ranking until the minority opinion could agree that at least that ranking might be proper.

As it turned out, the gun had a higher ranking than we had anticipated. Its use in survival was when a search plane came over: if it came over at night the gun could be fired so that sound could attract a rescue—something the other nine members of the group never considered.

So consensus is the most powerful forecasting system, but it's also the most expensive. Companies that forecast the sales of commercial airliners probably should use Focus Forecasting as a start and consensus for the finishing touches.

The Forecast Administrator

Many companies when they purchase a new forecasting system from one of the major software houses at the same time hire a forecast administrator. Unfortunately, most of what the forecast administrator does is put forecasts into the forecasting system. A lot of what the forecasting administrator does is a waste of time.

Here's what a forecast administrator should do:

1. Test the forecast outputs. He should look at the reasonability of the forecast, but if there is a chance that the forecast is right he should leave it alone. If the forecast is totally unreasonable, he should research with the forecast software supplier how these forecasts are arrived at. The system for generating the forecast should be changed, rather than just changing the forecast number.
2. Get information that the system doesn't have from marketing, from the customer, from Merchandising, from Design, from people who will influence the outcome of the forecast. He should channel this information into the forecast. Ideally, he should channel the information in as special requirement as part of DRP rather than modifying the gross forecast numbers.
3. Make every effort to make sure that the system is doing the forecasting. How else can a company learn to rely on a forecasting system in good times and in bad?
4. Compare the item forecast product class recap percent mix to the past sales class recap percent mix.
5. Create systems to eliminate order entry errors at the item customer-order-entry level.
6. Prepare a summary reconciliation of the difference between the company sales forecast and the item demand forecast from Focus Forecasting.
7. Use the histogram to come up with the best mix of formulas for the company and periodically check on the formula mix selection.
8. Any time a special requirement is added to Focus Forecasting or an item forecast is changed make sure there is documentation of why the forecast was changed.

The forecast administrator's main job is to maintain the integrity of the forecasting system, not to make forecasts to put into the forecast system.

Special Forecast Considerations

This chapter looked at special forecast considerations such as promotion items, seasonal items, lumpy demand items, dependent demand items, and discontinued items. It reviewed longer-term forecasts, management overrides, rules of thumb, and forecasting in bad times. It discussed a couple of systems for forecasting new items—the ranking system and consensus. It suggested duties for a forecast administrator.

Now, how do you use the power of Focus Forecasting to manage inventory? The best way is to use it to provide the mechanical part of the gross requirements for DRP.

PART III

Chapter Eleven

DRP—the Concept

DRP is a scheduling system. It looks like this:

DRP

0149   Black & Decker Items for our Chicago Warehouse

151021 3/8" Drill   Lead Time Wks 3 Safety Time Wks 1.5

	Now	Oct 08	Oct 15	Oct 22	Oct 29	Nov 05 etc
Gross Reqs	0	45	45	45	65	65
Sched Recs	0	0	0	0	72	0
Proj Onhand	120	75	30	-15	98	98
Planned Orders	0	106	65	65	65	65

Need by Oct-22 Scheduled Receipts through Oct-29

Here are DRP objectives:
1. Improve customer service
2. Improve inventory turnover
3. Increase aggregate gross profit
4. Reduce cost of operations
5. Improve the quality of business life

Here's what it does:

1. Orders inventory
2. Cancels and reduces excess inventory
3. Tells factories and suppliers about future orders
4. Allocates scarce inventory
5. Identifies excess inventory
6. Redistributes excess inventory
7. Provides summary measures of performance
8. Projects resource needs in value, weight, cube, hours, etc.
9. Uses exception reporting
10. Does break bulk allocations
11. Gets steady input from major customers
12. Creates action messages
13. Matches service-turnover needs to capacity
14. Converts customer item numbers to ours
15. Does joint replenishment for trucks, cars, and containers
16. Handles multiplant multiwarehouse inventory management
17. Provides input for EDI (Electronic Data Interchange)
18. Allows using JIT (Just in Time) logic effectively

For Manufacturing Companies

Currently most manufacturers with multiple plants and/or multiple distribution centers incorrectly plan production against a forecast of total customer demand. They use reorder points or order-up-tos to distribute product from the plant to the distribution centers. The problem is the sum of the orders to replenish the distribution centers never comes close to the total customer demand forecast, so that the plant makes the wrong goods at the wrong time.

The correct procedure is to forecast what the distribution center will ship to the customer. Use DRP to calculate future distribution center replenishment needs from the plant. Use DRP to tell the plant what production to plan for the future based on distribution center replenishment needs rather than forecasts of what distribution centers will ship out to the customers.

For Wholesalers

Most wholesalers and retailers treat their supplie⌐ They beat them for the best price. They surprise ther orders or no purchase orders. They beat them to exp large quantities of randomly selected items. They use reorder poinls or order-up-tos to launch purchase orders, expecting their supplier to have an infinite supply on hand. They promote the supplier's goods at random intervals. They use alternate suppliers because their regular supplier can't deliver. No wonder!

Wholesalers and mass merchants should use DRP to purchase from suppliers. They should use DRP to give the supplier advance notice of what they will be ordering in the future. Here are the advantages:

1. Suppliers will ship 100 percent complete.
2. Suppliers will give added discounts.
3. Suppliers won't have to carry safety stock to cover their own forecast errors.
4. Wholesalers and mass merchants won't have to carry safety stock to cover supplier delivery failures.

One wholesaler, who switched from reorder points to DRP, reported in their annual report that on the DRP vendors they experienced a 25 percent increase in aggregate gross profit, a 42 percent annual sales increase, and a 15 percent reduction in inventory.

For Retailers

Multiple store retailers can use DRP to reorder for the stores from their warehouses. Then they can use DRP to order from their suppliers. Moreover, retailers can use DRP to order fashion goods as well as basic goods. DRP can use its capacity planning concept to allow retailers who buy fashion lines or lines of closeouts to fit in specific item purchase programs to satisfy open-to-buy parameters.

DRP at the retail level has the following potential benefits:

1. Quick response systems that really work
2. Improving gross margin return on inventory
3. Reducing excess inventory sold at markdown prices
4. Providing customer supplier connectivity

Sadly, retailers are usually the last industry to start using a new technology. Only the giant mass merchants at this time recognize the potential of DRP in retail.

Inventory Management Problems

This book is about Focus Forecasting and DRP. Where should you start? Having worked with almost two hundred different companies in the past five years, Christopher and I believe there is no question. DRP is the place to start. Here is a list of inventory management problems that may be part of your company's problems. Some inventory management systems approximate the movement of goods with averages, reorder points, and summary numbers like total on order. DRP displays the physical movement of goods and so highlights the priority inventory management problems in the company. Every company we worked with initially felt their priority problem was inability to forecast accurately. Just about every company that started with DRP found this was not true. It was one of these other problems:

1. Bad records
2. Lead time inconsistency
3. Management refusing to take action
4. Quality problems
5. Common carriers piling up goods at terminals
6. Goods stuck on the receiving dock
7. Marketing running random unannounced promotions
8. Bad ship pack numbers
9. No excess inventory disposal
10. Volume buying for better gross
11. Infrequent inventory review
12. Order-filling errors
13. Ignoring joint replenishment

14. Reserving inventory
15. Slow transfers
16. Major customer killer surprise orders
17. Repair parts usage
18. Pilferage
19. Slow return-goods processing
20. Terrible computer systems
21. Protecting complicated job prestige
22. Timing shipments to meet financial goals
23. Vendor short-term selection based on price only
24. Unrealistic goals
25. No backup center shipments allowed
26. Overemphasis on cost control
27. No management return on investment (ROI) and/or customer service measures
28. Data base inflexible integrated systems
29. Lack of training
30. Knee-jerk MIS work

and finally

31. Poor forecasting

These problems are usually hidden in the finished goods inventory management in the company. DRP holds the problem up to the light so the company can fix it or purposely ignore it. Fixing these problems highlighted by DRP and the installation of DRP are a large part of the company success stories in the appendix of this book.

Next here's how we got involved in DRP in the first place.

Chapter Twelve

DRP—the History

Ollie and I had finished discussing Focus Forecasting. Later, while munching hamburgers on his floating barbecue boat on Lake Sunapee, he said, "There is one more thing you should be doing at American Hardware; DRP. Up at Abbott Labs Andre Martin and I have been using some of the MRP logic on finished goods with some great results. Why should you, Bernie, just surprise your suppliers with orders from a reorder point system? Why not use DRP to give them schedules of what you plan to buy in the future?"

I was too young and too dumb to understand the significance of what he was telling me at the time. I made a half hearted attempt at manually buying from Black & Decker using DRP logic, and I incorporated a chapter on basic DRP concepts in my 1978 book on Focus Forecasting.

The last three inventory managers at American Hardware before me had only lasted two years each. The Focus Forecasting program and reorder points served me well. By 1984 I had lasted thirteen years and really only had one major problem: I couldn't give the warehouse vice president accurate forecasts of what goods would be arriving on the dock next month. I couldn't even come close. I'd forecast $22 million and $14 million would arrive. Operations would run major idle capacity hours. I'd forecast $14 million and $22 million would arrive. Operations would run major overtime and wind up with goods piled up on the receiving docks, hurting service levels.

The operations manager was a bull of a man and always looked like he would like to kill me in our monthly Bickerson meetings. I called my friend Andre Martin and told him I wanted to use DRP a little bit. I just wanted to use it to help me forecast inbound for the warehouses. We decided to try DRP out on seven vendors on a microcomputer system that I would personally code myself. We picked the seven of my three thousand suppliers who were major problems already so we could not get in too much trouble.

The results were outstanding. We increased sales; we increased gross profit; we reduced inventory. We got added 1 percent from a number of the vendors. We projected that we could add an extra umpteen million dollars to the bottom line if we put all of American Hardware's vendors on DRP. Of course at the time all we had was a Radio Shack TRS 80 with a tape cassette to use. We needed major MIS support to either automate creation of the data for the micro system or program DRP on the mainframe. MIS was tied up. MIS stayed tied up until August of 1986. By then I knew the potential of DRP and was totally frustrated we couldn't move forward.

In August of 1986 I formed B. T. Smith and Associates to work exclusively in the area of DRP paperless inventory management systems. By November of 1987 I had thirty customers. I was on top of the world. I was in France riding a train back from Kodak in Chalon-sur-Saone to Paris when I couldn't stand the pain anymore and flew back to the United States for surgery. I had cancer of the pancreas and believed I would surely die.

My oldest son, Christopher, took over as president of B. T. Smith and Associates. I had written the initial DRP in Basic. It worked, but it looked like Dad's software.

Christopher rewrote it in fourth-generation C Language . . . user friendly, color screens, function keys, windows, AS400 interface, and all those other goodies. He now runs B. T. Smith and Associates, with DRP installations in over four hundred locations worldwide. I work for him as a consultant. Knock on wood, I'm still feisty enough to give most companies as much abrasive dissent as they care for. The next part of the book is about the detailed lessons we've learned in DRP installations in over 140 companies.

Chapter Thirteen

DRP Definitions

In a manufacturing company here's a typical DRP network:

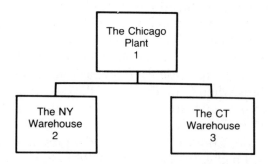

The Chicago plant makes goods for shipment direct to customers and for shipment to the New York and Connecticut warehouses.

DRP   NY Warehouse   0002

151021 3/8" Drill   Lead Time Wks 1   Safety Time Wks1.5

	Now	Oct 08	Oct 15	Oct 22	Oct 29	Nov 05	etc
Gross Reqs	0	45	45	45	65	65	
Sched Recs	0	0	0	0	0	0	
Proj Onhand	120	75	78	98	98	98	
Planned Orders	0	48	65	65	65	65	

Release Planned Order

Release Planned Order

Our New York warehouse has 120 drills on hand. The lead time from the time we place an order on the Chicago plant finished goods inventory until the goods are available for sale from New York is 1 period. We try to keep a minimum of 1.5 periods' supply on hand in New York.

Some Definitions

Gross Requirements

Gross requirements is an expression of what we must ship out from the New York warehouse to customers period by period into the future. It can come from a number of procedures or a combination of any of them in the form of mechanical forecasts or statements of special requirements:

1. Forecasts:
   a. Focus Forecasting or some other mechanical forecast
   b. Customer forecasts of future purchases
   c. Salesman or marketing estimates of future sales
2. Special requirements:
   a. Backorders we owe our customers
   b. Orders from our customers for future shipment
   c. Upcoming promotions or special events
   d. Transfers that New York has not yet deducted from the New York inventory to ship to the Connecticut warehouse

Scheduled Receipts

1. On order from the plant with the expected delivery date for orders that have already been printed on paper but not yet received from the plant.
2. Transfers from the Connecticut warehouse to New York with the expected delivery date for transfers that have already been printed on paper but not yet received from the Connecticut warehouse.

Projected On-Hand

The current available balance, taking into account gross requirements, scheduled receipts, and planned orders period by period out into the future.

Planned Orders

1. The orders DRP calculates we must release each period into the future in order to satisfy the lead time and safety time parameters we told DRP to use.
2. Firm-planned orders that override the DRP calculation of planned orders.

Action Messages

1. Release planned order . . . make a purchase right now.
2. Need by xx/xx scheduled receipts through xx/xx.
3. Reduce or cancel scheduled receipts this quantity through xx/xx.

This is the basic DRP information, no matter whether we are using it at the retail, wholesale, or manufacturing level. In the next chapter we will see how manufacturers typically operate DRP to manage inventory.

Chapter Fourteen

DRP Operating Procedures

In a Manufacturing Company

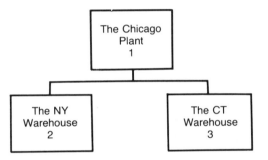

The Chicago plant makes goods for shipment direct to customers and for shipment to the New York and Connecticut warehouses.

DRP   NY Warehouse   0002

151021 3/8" Drill   Lead Time Wks 1   Safety Time Wks 1.5

	Now	Oct 08	Oct 15	Oct 22	Oct 29	Nov 05	etc
Gross Reqs	0	45	45	45	65	65	
Sched Recs	0	0	0	0	0	0	
Proj Onhand	120	75	78	98	98	98	
Planned Orders	0	48	65	65	65	65	

Release Planned Order

Our New York warehouse has 120 drills on hand. The lead time from the time we place an order on the Chicago plant finished goods inventory until the goods are available for sale from New York is 1 week. We try to keep a minimum of 1.5 weeks' supply on hand in New York.

DRP is a system that manages inventory. It is not a system that provides information for managing inventory. Management sets the parameters; lead time, safety time, ship pack, message threshold, joint replenishment minimums, etc. DRP uses these parameters to create planned orders and to direct expedite and delay and reduce activity. It should really work if it is set up right. The planner should only override the system about 1 percent of the time.

If we can send robot photographic rocket probes to Neptune, why can't we have a simple automated inventory management system? Let the computer do the arithmetic. Let the planner or buyer do the Sherlock Holmes work when things go wrong.

The Operating Procedure . . . the Big Picture

In a manufacturing company a typical DRP operating procedure will have the following steps:

1. Run summary measures of performance
   a. Inventory level,
   b. Total upcoming gross requirements,
   c. Projected turnover,
   d. Number of out-of-stocks, and/or
   e. Projected fill rate.
2. Post the summary measures to track progress.
3. Work DRP for individual items.
   a. Approve or disagree with DRP's suggested orders.
   b. Approve or disagree with DRP move-up or delay messages.
4. Summarize planned orders to create gross requirements on the plant
   If the plant normally will have goods available, go to step 6.
5. Allocate plant on hand and upcoming finished production.
6. Create purchase orders for this period's shipments from the plant.

7. Transmit the purchase orders to the plant or print the purchase orders and mail them to the plant.
8. Work DRP at the plant level to critique the Master Production Schedule, looking at:
   a. Customer service,
   b. Turnover, and
   c. Utilization of machine and labor capacity.
9. Update the master production schedule and send it to MRP.
10. Analyze excess inventory by branch periodically every two to three months and reallocate inventories to balance excesses.
11. Save the DRP decisions magnetically so sometimes we can revisit how we caused the ten worst excesses or ten worst out-of-stocks in the company.

The Operating Procedure . . . in Detail

In detail, this is what those DRP steps look like:

Before working any distribution center for a detail DRP item, the inventory planner should look at summary measures of performance to make sure the system is not running the company down a rat hole. In DRP this can be accomplished by tracking select figures from twelve period projections for all of the items in the New York warehouse:

The planner should post these key summary figures for New York every week to chart inventory management progress or lack of progress.

Lots of companies want to automate this manual record keeping for the inventory planner. But it's better to rub the planner's nose in the numbers to make sure the planner considers the trend of each figure. For example:

1. If the inventory beginning figure is exactly the same for New York for two weeks in a row, somebody in Data Processing forgot to update the on hand.
2. If the inventory beginning figure jumps up or down 20 percent, somebody fouled up stating this week's inventory figures. Inventories generally like to change only a little bit at a time.

12 Period Summary
0002 NY Warehouse
0001 Chicago Source
In Value
Oct 8 xxxx

Lead Time Wks: var   Safety Time Wks: var

	On Hand	Gross Reqs	Sched Recs	Planned Orders
Beg Fig	$ 658,919			
Now	1,300,780	0	641,861	196,386
Oct-08	1,161,760	165,165	26,145	735,599
Oct-15	996,594	165,165	0	186,837
Oct-22	1,679,125	249,454	0	220,185
Oct-29	1,618,126	247,835	0	245,001
Nov-05	1,590,476	247,835	0	161,594
Nov-12	1,587,642	247,835	0	165,564
		etc.		
Total	$1,347,762	2,776,554	668,006	2,910,232

Turns 8.17 # of outs 695   # of items 1,423   Fill rate 86.7%

NY Warehouse Summary Performance

Date	Beg On Hand	Gross Reqs	Proj Turns	Fill Rate
Oct-01	$ 569,341	2,544,344	9.36	84.2%
Oct-08	658,919	2,776,554	8.17	86.7
		etc.		

3. If the gross requirements are exactly the same as last week, some-body didn't give us the new customer backorders or orders for future shipment or reduce or add to the promotion events still outstanding.
4. If the gross requirements change more than 20 percent in one week, either somebody fouled up the record keeping or Sales and Marketing have had a celestial visitation during the week.
5. If the projected turnover is too high we have to allow a safety time setting and will surely run the company out of stock and shut down a few plants along the way.
6. If the fill rates keep going down, we don't have the safety time set high enough or we are not using the DRP system properly.

The first thing we do when a company asks us to audit the performance of their DRP system is to ask to see their 12 period summary postings. If they are not posting the 12 period summary figures they should not be surprised if DRP doesn't do anything posi-tive for their inventory management. Any DRP system requires sum-mary measures of performance as a first step and as a consistent part of the DRP process.

Working DRP

Working DRP means:

DRP   NY Warehouse   0002

151021 3/8" Drill   Lead Time Wks 1   Safety Time Wks 1.5

	Now	Oct 08	Oct 15	Oct 22	Oct 29	Nov 05	etc
Gross Reqs	0	45	45	45	65	65	
Sched Recs	0	0	0	0	0	0	
Proj Onhand	120	75	78	98	98	98	
Planned Orders	0	48	65	65	65	65	

Release Planned Order

1. Approving or disagreeing with planned orders
2. Approving or disagreeing with expedite messages
3. Approving or disagreeing with reduce or cancel messages

In the example above, DRP calculated a planned order for forty-eight drills. If the planner agrees with DRP's order, he just asks for the next action message item in New York. Only if the planner disagrees with the calculated planned order should the planner override DRP's calculation with a firm-planned order. In the firm-planned order, the planner should state what was wrong with DRP's original planned order, for example:

1. Fall promo not in gross requirements
2. Ship pack should be 72
3. This item to be discontinued

The input to DRP should be changed to reflect the problem so DRP does not make the same mistake next time. Why did the planner know about the fall promo if DRP didn't know? Why is the ship pack wrong? Why hasn't the item been coded as no-buy discontinued?

When the system is set up right, the planner will agree with the calculated planned orders by just asking for the next action item.

DRP   NY Warehouse   0002

151021 3/8" Drill   Lead Time Wks 1   Safety Time Wks 1.5

	Now	Oct 08	Oct 15	Oct 22	Nov 05	etc
Gross Reqs	0	45	45	45	65	65
Sched Recs	0	5000	0	0	0	0
Proj Onhand	120	5075	5030	4985	4920	4855
Planned Orders	0	0	0	0	0	0

SR S-PO W00150527 for 5000;   10-03-xx by 10-08-xx

Reduce scheduled receipts through Nov 05 this quantity 4790

Delay Messages

DRP is telling the plant to reduce the 5000-drill order to just 210 units. If the planner agrees, he just asks for the next action item.

If the planner disagrees because he knows there is a fall promo coming up, he puts in a comment saying: "Do not reduce this order. We need it for fall promo." Of course DRP should already have known about the fall promo as part of special requirements. If the fall promo were in as a special requirement DRP would not have suggested reducing the scheduled receipt in the first place.

DRP   NY Warehouse   0002

151021 3/8" Drill   Lead Time Wks 1   Safety Time Wks 1.5

	Now	Oct 08	Oct 15	Oct 22	Oct 29	Nov 05	etc
Gross Reqs	0	45	45	45	65	65	
Sched Recs	0	0	0	0	72	0	
Proj Onhand	120	75	30	26	98	98	
Planned Orders	0	0	41	65	65	65	

Release Planned Order

SR S-PO W00150527 for 72;   10-03-xx by 10-29-xx

Need by Oct-22 Scheduled receipts through Oct-29

Expedite Orders

If the planner agrees that the plant should speed up delivery of this order if it can, then the planner just asks for the next DRP action item. If the plant had already responded that it could not speed up delivery, their notation would appear on the scheduled receipt as a comment.

If the system is working right, the planner will agree with most of the DRP actions indicated. If not, the DRP system should be changed so the planner does not keep fixing the same problems every week.

Summarizing Planned Orders

After the planners have posted 12 period summaries and worked DRP for both New York and Connecticut, DRP can summarize the planned orders from each of these warehouses to create gross requirements on the Chicago plant.

Generating the Purchase or Orders from the Plant

At this point, especially in start-up DRP environment, the planner can use DRP to allocate existing plant on hand and upcoming completed production orders to the New York and Connecticut distribution centers. The output from these allocations can be used to create the purchase orders for this period's shipments from the plant to the distribution centers.

Of course if goods are normally available, the planner can use DRP to just release the planned orders for regular lead time and for rush orders. This is the simplest form of DRP. Once DRP has been operating for a while, the plant probably will have the goods available when they are needed.

DRP can create paperless purchase orders that can be sent to the plant electronically to fill. Or DRP could print purchase orders to mail to the plant.

DRP   The Chicago Plant 0001

151021 3/8" Drill   Lead Time Wks 0   Safety Time Wks 0

	Now	Oct 08	Oct 15	Oct 22	Oct 29	Nov 05	etc
Gross Reqs	24	48	48	24	48	24	
Sched Recs	0	0	0	0	0	0	
Proj Onhand	16	-2	-20	-14	-32	-26	
Planned Orders	0	30	30	30	30	30	

SR P-PO MPSW00150527 for 30; 10-08-xx by 10-08-xx
SR P-PO MPSW00150528 for 30; 10-15-xx by 10-15-xx

Need by Oct-08 Scheduled Receipts through Oct-15

Critiquing the Master Production Schedule

DRP is saying that the Master Production Schedule on this item should be accelerated one week.

Rebalance Excess Inventories

DRP can identify items in a distribution center that has on hand quantities over a certain number of months' supply and worth more than a certain value. The planner can use DRP to identify these excesses and to reallocate the inventory to the proper center, avoiding additional production.

Rebalancing inventory should only occur on a regular scheduled basis every two or three months to relieve excesses. Planners should not be rebalancing inventory every time there is a potential out-of-stock or every time the Master Production Schedule is prepared. Rebalancing inventory creates chaos in a company. It should happen infrequently and only for significant excesses. It should take into account the additional cost of operation created in the transfer and in the record keeping and control.

Push or Pull

Some companies don't make what they sell. They sell what they make. This is true of cigarettes, dog food, chocolate bars, and other products where the manufacture of the product is the key element. The machine must run at all times. Places must be found to ship the outcoming production.

DRP also operates in these companies by using its break bulk feature to allocate where goods coming out of production should be shipped to keep the inventory distributed generally in line with forecasted sales.

This procedure is similar to companies that are not sure of product availability at the plant and therefore must run allocations before creating paperwork for this week's shipments.

In the next chapter we will look at DRP for wholesaler inventory management.

Chapter Fifteen

DRP Operating Procedures

In a Wholesaling Company

The reason these DRP procedures are so automatic is that my experience was in a company that handled 165,000 stock-keeping units. I couldn't put up with a system that provided information to manage inventory. I needed a system that managed inventory. In my wholesale business either the automatic system worked or you got a new system. There was no time to make manual decisions on so many thousands of items.

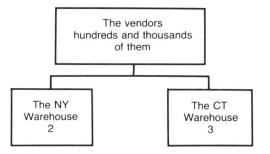

The vendors make goods for shipment direct to the wholesaler's customers and for shipment to the wholesaler's New York and Connecticut warehouses.

6921 Black & Decker
151021 3/8" Drill   Lead Time Wks 1   Safety Time Wks 1.5

	Now	Oct 08	Oct 15	Oct 22	Oct 29	Nov 05	etc
Gross Reqs	0	45	45	45	65	65	
Sched Recs	0	0	0	0	0	0	
Proj Onhand	120	75	78	98	98	98	
Planned Orders	0	48	65	65	65	65	

Release Planned Order

Our New York warehouse has 120 drills on hand. The lead time from the time we place an order on the Black & Decker supplier inventory until the goods are available for sale from New York is 1 week. We try to keep a minimum of 1.5 weeks' supply on hand in NY.

The Operating Procedure . . . the Big Picture

In a wholesaling company a typical DRP operating procedure will have the following steps:

1. Run summary measures by vendor of
   a. Inventory level,
   b. Total upcoming gross requirements,
   c. Projected turnover,
   d. Number of out-of-stocks, and/or
   e. Projected fill rate.
2. Post the summary measures to track progress.
3. Work DRP for individual items.
   a. Approve or disagree with DRP's suggested orders.
   b. Approve or disagree with DRP move-up or delay messages.
4. Run summaries of total order dimensions from a vendor to create a total mix of products to meet restrictions such as:
   a. Container load, carload, truckload, or prepaid freight load.
   b. Weight, pounds, cube, or number of pallets or value for special-order-size bonus discounts.

5. Create purchase orders for this period's purchases from the vendor

6. Transmit the purchase orders to the vendor or print the purchase orders and mail them to the vendor

7. Work with vendors to speed up or delay selected items on outstanding purchase orders

8. Summarize planned orders for individual distribution centers on to a dummy distribution center:

    a. Use the summary total to project future planned orders in total for items to the vendor

    b. Use the summary total to order in bulk from the vendor and only decide individual distribution center breakdown when goods arrive by allocating and cross-docking

9. Analyze excess inventory by branch periodically every two or three months and reallocate inventories to balance excesses

10. Negotiate price discounts and delivery guarantees in exchange for firm-planned order periods and consistent updates of future planned order

The Operating Procedure . . . in Detail

In detail this is what those DRP steps look like:

Wholesalers can have thousands of items and hundreds and thousands of vendors. Usually the management of inventory of these items is organized by product lines. Usually some portion of the total number of vendors is reviewed for ordering on a selected day during the week. It is necessary to review all of the items for a supplier at the same time because of joint replenishment considerations such as prepaid freight on truckload shipments. For a buyer a detail operating procedure might look like this:

1. DRP runs a 12 period summary for each of the vendors selected for review this day of the week.

2. As a first step the buyer posts the summary figures for each vendor:

12 Period Summary
Vendor   6921 Black & Decker
Our Center   0002 NY Warehouse
In Value
Oct 8 xxxx

Lead Time Wks: Var   Safety Time Wks: Var

	On Hand	Gross Reqs	Sched Recs	Planned Orders
Beg Fig	$ 658,919			
Now	1,300,780	0	641,861	196,386
Oct-08	1,161,760	165,165	26,145	735,599
Oct-15	996,594	165,165	0	186,837
Oct-22	1,679,125	249,454	0	220,185
Oct-29	1,618,126	247,835	0	245,001
Nov-05	1,590,476	247,835	0	161,594
Nov-12	1,587,642	247,835	0	165,564
		etc.		
Total	$1,347,762	2,776,554	668,006	2,910,232

Turns 8.17 #of Outs 695   #of Items 1,423   Fill Rate 86.7%

NY Warehouse Summary Performance
Black & Decker 6921

Date	Beg On Hand	Gross Reqs	Proj Turns	Fill Rate
Oct-01	$ 569,341	2,544,344	9.36	84.2%
Oct-08	658,919	2,776,554	8.17	86.7
		etc.		

3. Work DRP for each item in each warehouse regardless of the vendor who will ultimately ship the goods.
    a. Approve or disagree with DRP's suggested orders.
    b. Approve or disagree with DRP's move-up or delay messages.
4. Use DRP to show planned order totals by vendor matching the vendor's restriction in the vendor's terms against the planned order total.
    a. Planned order total: 19.5 pallets
    b. Minimum freight prepaid: 22.0 pallets

DRP says try a safety time of 4.26 weeks to meet the vendor restriction.

Keep iterating until the joint replenishment order from the vendor meets the restriction or the weeks of supply required are too high a price to pay for prepaid shipment.

DRP can now generate a purchase order for individual items totaling to the vendor's restriction.

5. Create purchase orders to transmit to the vendor or to print and mail to the vendor.
    a. Create separate purchases for emergency shipment or
    b. Combine emergency shipments with the regular order.
6. Use DRP to communicate to vendors the desired speedup or delay of outstanding purchase orders.
    a. Send DRP expedite or delay reports to vendors over EDI or print and mail schedule change requests.
    b. Record vendor comments and change expected deliveries and quantities in line with vendor discussions.

Remember that the most effective expediting is to try to cancel a late outstanding order. It's almost always just been shipped out the door.

7. Use DRP to summarize planned orders for all of our warehouses into a dummy consolidation center.
    a. This summary center will show the total requirement for an item and for a vendor throughout our DRP network.

b. If we generate orders for the summary center, it can be any one of our regular centers. When the goods arrive we can use DRP to allocate how the goods should be distributed to individual centers and cross-dock the goods in one door and out the other without double handling.

c. If we import it can take three to six months for a container to arrive domestically. This procedure allows us to decide final distribution of goods after we have learned more about actual sales distribution.

8. Use DRP to analyze and redistribute excess inventories every two or three months.

a. Some buyers try to utilize excess inventories every time before they write a new order on a vendor. This practice can keep their company in a constant state of chaos, and they can wind up with goods floating around the country on a truck while being out of stock in every warehouse. It's much better to systematically redistribute major overstocks infrequently, taking into account the cost of double handling, record keeping, and joint replenishment freight considerations.

b. To cover out-of-stocks it's better to have the order entry system ship from a backup warehouse than to try to transfer goods between warehouses to head off out-of-stocks. The order entry system should still record the demand history from the original warehouse the item was supposed to be from.

9. Use DRP to negotiate with vendors. Do not just give them the DRP planned order information. Without a contract the process of communicating future order information is worse than worthless.

a. Both the customer and the vendor can win if it's set up properly. The customer won't need safety stock to cover vendor delivery failure. The vendor won't need safety stock to cover forecast errors.

b. The customer's considerations given in the contract are: A firm planned order period the customer must accept orders within if pressed.

A consistent (monthly) update of future planned orders sent to the vendor.

A concentration of ordering with the selected vendor. No shopping around for best price on every order.

c. The vendor's considerations given are:
   A discount on purchases across-the-board.
   A guarantee of 100 percent service with freight prepaid air shipments of backorders.
   A consistent adherence to a negotiated lead time, not earlier, not later.

At one wholesaler on seven selected vendors the rewards using this DRP approach were:

1. A 44 percent sales increase
2. A 25 percent gross profit increase
3. A 15 percent inventory reduction

In the next chapter we'll look at how a retailer can use DRP.

Chapter Sixteen

DRP Retailer Operating Procedures

As part of my job at Warner's World Famous Girdles and Bras I set up retail inventory replenishment systems for 150 major department stores for our products across the United States. At American Hardware I worked with giant chains and little mom-and-pop stores to improve inventory management. That's part of this chapter on the use of DRP in retailing.

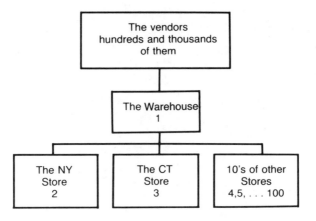

The vendors make goods for shipment direct to the retailer's stores and for shipment to the retailer's warehouse for shipment to the stores.

6921 Black & Decker
151021 3/8" Drill   Lead Time Wks 1   Safety Time Wks 1.5

	Now	Oct 08	Oct 15	Oct 22	Oct 29	Nov 05	etc
Gross Reqs	0	5	4	0	6	5	
Sched Recs	0	0	0	0	0	0	
Proj Onhand	20	15	11	11	12	10	
Planned Orders	0	0	0	7	3	6	

Up until the use of bar codes, universal product codes, and other source marking techniques it was virtually impossible for retailers to keep reasonably accurate records of on-hand balances in their stores. It is still impossible for at least half the retail stores in the world because of their lack of discipline, low-paid help, and thousands of low-sales-volume items.

For those who can achieve reasonable on-hand balance records DRP can work wonders for improving sales, gross profit, and gross margin return on inventory. DRP can raise GMROI from a feeble 1.1 to 1.8 and better. GMROI is your annual gross profit divided by your average inventory investment. Any answer less than 1 and you are probably going out of business.

A number of progressive vendors are offering to manage retail inventories of their products knowing that healthier customers mean better business for the vendors themselves. A number of progressive mass merchants are starting to use DRP to manage their retail inventories and to develop quick response systems with their suppliers.

The Operating Procedure . . . the Big Picture

In a retailing company a typical DRP operating procedure will have the following steps:

1. Run summary measures:
   a. Inventory level,
   b. Total upcoming gross requirements,
   c. Projected turnover,

    d. Number of out-of-stocks, and/or
    e. Projected fill rate.

They run these measures by store if buyers are responsible for replenishment of the whole store or by store within product class if merchants are responsible for their lines in all stores.

2. Post the summary measures to track progress.
3. Work DRP for individual items.
    a. Approve or disagree with DRP's suggested orders.
    b. Approve or disagree with DRP's move-up or delay messages.
4. Create orders for this period's required replenishment from the warehouse and for purchase orders directly on the vendor.
5. Transmit the orders to the warehouse or print the purchase orders and mail them to the warehouse.
6. Summarize planned orders for individual stores on to the warehouse.
    a. Use DRP to buy from vendors at the warehouse level.
    b. Use DRP to buy in bulk from the vendor and only decide individual store breakdown when goods arrive by allocating and cross-docking.
7. Work with vendors to speed up or delay selected items on outstanding purchase orders.
8. Analyze excess inventory by store periodically every two to three months and reallocate inventories to balance excesses.
9. Negotiate price discounts and delivery guarantees in exchange for firm-planned order periods and consistent updates of future planned orders.
10. Make up quick response systems with participating vendors to maximize inventory turnover throughout the store group.

DRP can operate in retail where the retailer is in the fashion or category business even if the individual items are not normally reordered for more than one season. It has the ability to do product line or product group planning, allowing the buyer to fill in the detail purchases with specific items and selected vendors. The details of this procedure go beyond the scope of this book.

There are very few retailers at this moment using DRP. The potential to use DRP as an overwhelming competitive edge is there. We only know of five retailers involved in DRP as of the writing of this book. Their success will prompt more interest in the future.

Chapter Seventeen

Creating the DRP Data Base

The most successful DRP systems are paperless. After all, the information presented for one item on DRP is about twenty times as lengthy as a reorder point report for the same item. If you print out DRP long-term your system is doomed to failure.

The most powerful paperless DRP systems run on microcomputers hooked to file servers. Running DRP on a microcomputer allows DRP to recalculate planned orders and reanalyze data for action messages as the planner or buyer works on the DRP screen. The LAN (Local Area Network) and the WAN (Wide Area Network) hooking multiple microcomputers to a central data base on a file server give the user the flexibility of a microcomputer with the integration of a mainframe.

Most company data bases are on mainframe or minicomputers. It's dangerous to build separate microcomputer data bases that can fall out of sync with the mainframe. It's dangerous because people can then come to management meetings with conflicting sets of data from the two systems. For this reason, when companies tap the mainframe data base for the file server it is wise to bring down all of the data fresh at this moment in time. Don't just update the information on the file server. Treat the file server and the microcomputers as if they were blank chalkboards. Bring the entire data base to the DRP micro system before operating the system.

Here are the data base elements required for a DRP system:

Forecasts

1. Focus Forecasting or some other mechanical forecast.
2. Customer forecasts for future purchases.
3. Salesman or marketing estimates of future sales.

6921 Black & Decker
151021 3/8" Drill   Lead Time Wks 1   Safety Time Wks 1.5

	Now	Oct 08	Oct 15	Oct 22	Oct 29	Nov 05	etc
Gross Reqs	0	45	45	45	65	65	
Sched Recs	0	0	0	0	0	0	
Proj Onhand	120	75	78	98	98	98	
Planned Orders	0	48	65	65	65	65	

Release Planned Order

Special Requirements

1. Backorders we owe our customers.
2. Orders from our customers for future shipment.
3. Upcoming promotions or special events.
4. Transfers that New York has not yet deducted from the New York inventory to ship to the Connecticut warehouse.

Scheduled Receipts

1. On order from the plant with the expected delivery date for orders that have already been printed on paper but not yet received from the plant.
2. Transfers from the Connecticut warehouse to New York with the expected delivery date for transfers that have already been printed on paper but not yet received from the Connecticut warehouse.

On-hand

The current physical on-hand balance.

Lead Time

The time it takes from when the planner approves the order on the DRP screen until it is on the shelf available for sale.

Safety Time

1. The desired end of each period inventory time supply in terms of future gross requirements.
2. DRP will convert this time supply to an inventory quantity.
3. This safety supply will cover low forecasts, low lead time parameters, and other inventory problems that would otherwise cause out-of-stock.

Ship Packs

1. The minimum order quantity . . . usually a box, pack, bag, pallet, or other manageable quantity of product.
2. DRP will make sure the planned order, if any, is at least this quantity.

Unit Value

A value DRP can use to show total value of inventory, gross requirements, scheduled receipts, and planned orders.

Unit Weight

A weight DRP can use to check whether shipping parameters—truckloads, carloads, container loads—have been met.

Unit Cube

1. A cubic extension DRP can use to see if the joint order will fit in the shipping container.
2. A cubic extension DRP can use to see how much warehouse space will be consumed.

Vendor Code

The ultimate source goods will come from as part of this DRP network. We may get this item from our warehouse 14, but warehouse 14 gets it from vendor code 6921.

Consolidation Center

The immediate source of this item. In the example above the consolidation center would be 14.

Item Description

How we describe this item—one-quart freezer bag, for example.

All of these data base items come from the company mainframe or minicomputer to feed the DRP system. A programmer on the mainframe or minicomputer must gather this data from the company data base and put it in the format that DRP can use. This is true whether the DRP system is a mainframe, minicomputer, or microcomputer system. The important thing is that the DRP data base is totally refreshed before the DRP operating procedure begins. A typical system can refresh fifteen thousand items in four minutes.

Chapter Eighteen

Special DRP Considerations

DRP Is Dull

When DRP systems are operating effectively they are deadly dull. It's much more fun to have a crisis at least once a day. It's more fun to feel your heart pound as the customer or company president chews you out for your current stupidity. It's exciting to make those emergency phone calls grabbing people from meetings or the cafeteria. It's exhilarating to get emergency fax messages from halfway around the world expediting goods. At the end of the day you know your job is important. No doubt management by chaos is more fun than routine DRP systems.

After all, if DRP is really a process guidance system that truly manages inventory, what does a planner or buyer who used to do complex multivariate simultaneous equation inventory management with a pencil . . . what does that person do?

DRP keeps track of each prior period's decisions. By analyzing the current ten worst out-of-stocks, ten worst overstocks, and ten most costly glitches, the planner or buyer can actually start to find out what the real inventory management problems in the company are. He can actually work toward changing policies and procedures to head off these problems in the future. After a while, he will find this procedure much more rewarding then second-guessing calculated planned orders and expediting mistakes of the past.

DRP Is Simple

Let's face it. Once you get the hang of calculating projected on-hand balances, you see that DRP logic is right up there with balancing your checkbook. Some people cannot stand this simplicity. Here's what they do to keep the water muddy:

1. Let's calculate economic lot sizes so we don't run up cost of handling in the warehouse. Let's make sure they are right before we start.

Result: DRP doubles inventory. DRP must be no good.

2. We must redo our data base first to ensure the integrity of the data we are giving DRP. After all, garbage in, garbage out.

Result: After ten or twenty years, entire company retires while new crew comes in to work on data base.

3. Obviously our problem is our forecast is wrong. We should start by getting a correct forecast.

Result: Company purchases new forecasting package, which also makes wrong forecasts. Repeat step 3.

4. We never know for sure if we will ship out of the warehouse or direct from the factory. It depends on the size of the customer's order.

Result: Two or three planners in the company are regarded as infinitely wise, but company stays on a manual system.

5. Our MIS group only allows UNIX base systems that run on Convergent Technology hardware.

Result: All-new systems cost six figures and take at least seven years to install.

6. DRP is just one small part of our overall solution. Our first step must address the human resource, quality, and integration of corporate culture issues.

Result: We have a lot of boring company meetings.

7. Can you calculate safety time by expected value of the logarithmic mean of the forecast error?

Result: We hire the president's Harvard Business School cousin for a year-and-a-half assignment.

8. We bottle water, beer, and shampoo. In that order. We don't want shampoo in our beer or beer in our water. Does DRP have a Smart/Expert system for sequencing lot sizes on multiple machines? This is our real problem.

Result: After a long period of inaction, the company goes into Chapter 11 bankruptcy.

9. We won't need DRP because we are installing JIT. We will be able to switch production and produce in such a short time period that we can just look at yesterday's results to see what we should do today.

Result: Operating costs go out of sight the minute the twenty-seven consultants monitoring the process leave the company plant.

DRP is like the skunkworks concept in the book *In Search of Excellence*. DRP is the place to start. It highlights with its action messages where the significant inventory management obstacles are in the company.

DRP and Focus Forecasting

Focus Forecasting is a great way to generate a mechanical forecast based on a demand history. This mechanical forecast is a major part of DRP gross requirements. When people put additional intelligence into Focus Forecasting such as upcoming promotions or events, those detail comments can carry forward into DRP as special requirements.

DRP can show in addition to gross requirements the past demand history. When the planner sees an unusual gross requirement projection in DRP related to the past history, the planner can also see the detail of the promotion influencing that forecast in the special requirements taken from Focus Forecasting.

Focus Forecasting is like the headlights on an inventory management car. DRP is the inventory management car.

DRP versus MRP

How is DRP different than MRP?

Multiplant, Multiwarehouse

DRP concerns itself primarily in managing inventory in multiple stocking locations or sourcing from multiple suppliers and/or plants. MRP allows a planner to schedule an item in a plant. DRP allows scheduling groups of items for multiple locations from multiple sources.

Allocations

DRP will take goods coming off a machine in a factory or a container load of goods coming in from a foreign country and determine where ideally those goods should be shipped at this time.

Allocations are of value:

1. Many companies import. Importing often has long lead times. It is better to decide where the goods ultimately will go when the container hits domestic soil.
2. Companies that have scarce production resources need to cover backorders and past due planned orders in multiple warehouses.
3. Companies that manufacture regardless of forecast demand need to know where to ship the goods when they come off the production line.

Joint Replenishment

DRP is concerned with the total of an order for a mix of products. Did we make forty-four thousand pounds of freight prepaid? Did we cube out with fourteen thousand furnace filters? Are there twenty-two pallets? Did we hit the twenty-thousand dollar extra 2 percent January special bonus offer? These are the questions DRP answers. It tells us how much of each item on the order we will need to meet the joint replenishment restriction. It's far better for us to decide what will fill the truck than to have some consolidator randomly fill the truck with items that simply take up the most room.

Finished Goods

Although DRP can calculate packaging requirements and other dependent related needs, DRP is usually used to maintain inventory of independent items like finished goods or replacement parts. At this time the following industries are using DRP: food, chemical, pharmaceutical, hardware, plastics, steel, automotive, electrical, plumbing, tools, apparel, communications, computer, retail, explosives, sporting goods and consumer products.

Schedule to Planned Orders

MRP usually has factory scheduling systems to support forecasts of total company outbound to the customers. DRP does factory scheduling against summary projections of planned orders needed to replenish company warehouses. DRP is usually a more accurate statement of factory requirements and current priorities.

MRP systems usually plan total production and use reorder point systems to distribute resultant finished goods. DRP displays the physical movement of goods from the factory through the distribution center to the customer. It ties together better the proper production schedules with the required future deployment of the goods.

Large Number of Skus

MRP is usually a people-intensive process where planners carefully review all of the elements of the planning process for a limited number of stock-keeping units. DRP automatically reviews tens and hundreds of thousands of items, only showing the buyer or planner the decisions of significant impact.

Manufacturers have hundreds of items in tens of places. Wholesalers have thousands of items in tens of places. Retailers have tens of thousands of items in hundreds of places. As the number of skus increase, the need for automated systems increase with less people review. DRP systems are usually less people-intensive than MRP systems.

Automated Forecast Input

MRP usually is using forecasts derived primarily from people input. These forecasts have heavy marketing and management interaction. That's okay with a limited number of items.

In a company using DRP to manage twenty thousand items in fifteen distribution centers the primary forecast driver must be an automatic system like Focus Forecasting. In those companies the only additional human input is information that is influenced by human interference with normal product flow, such as price discounts or special advertising of selected items.

Identifies and Redistributes Excess

Since DRP is by definition dealing with multiple inventory locations, it usually has the ability to identify and redistribute inventory excess. A person might ask DRP, for example, to display all on-hand quantities in excess of twelve weeks' supply and more than five thousand dollars in value.

Links to Nonmanufacturing Customers

The automotive industry employs MRP extensively. That industry can send raw planned orders to their suppliers to use as gross requirements. Retailers and wholesalers don't have MRP systems. DRP allows these nonmanufacturing companies to send their suppliers finished goods planned orders to use as gross requirements.

How is DRP like MRP?

Bill of Material Explosion

1. Like MRP, DRP systems can do infinite level bill of material explosions. It needs this ability to calculate end item purchase orders for items that are private-labeled or stocked in minor product variations.
2. DRP uses the bill of material explosion to allow rough-cut capacity planning for machine and work centers.
3. DRP uses the bill of materials to carry forward planned orders from items that are being phased out into the gross requirements of the new item.
4. DRP uses the bill of materials to sum up individual items to plan product category purchases.
5. DRP uses the bill of materials to convert from our customer's item number to our item number.

Paperless Purchasing

Like MRP, DRP operates on a cathode ray tube screen eliminating wheelbarrows full of eleven-by-fourteen-inch continuous forms from the mainframe computer.

Action Messages

DRP, just like MRP, suggests action messages:

1. Release planned orders
2. Expedite a scheduled receipt
3. Reduce or cancel a scheduled receipt

Powerful Scheduling Tools

Both MRP and DRP continually readjust the utilization of resources and the planned inventory balances to fit the new world that arises from each day's real events. Unless a process is entirely automated from knowing exactly what is required through acquisition of the raw materials, MRP and DRP systems will be needed to adjust to the real world.

Summary Measures

Both MRP and DRP can provide summary measures of inventory management progress. The real test is whether management has the courage to use the reports to reward and punish the people responsible for the numbers.

1. At least look at the summary measures.
2. Ask why the performance is at the current level.
3. Make the performance measures the major part of performance reviews for salary increase, promotion, demotion, and dismissal.

MRP Logic

Both MRP and DRP use precisely the same logic to calculate planned order quantities and to create action messages.

Networked

Both DRP and MRP can enjoy the advantages of intelligent terminals running on a network environment. The old dumb terminal configuration required complex mainframe or minicomputer programs to do all the calculations for multiple-user stations. The new networks are many times faster and yet still preserve the single data base utilization and integrity.

EDI

Both MRP and DRP are better solutions to electronic links between customers and suppliers. As Ollie Wight told me, it's far better to give a supplier a vision of future needs than to just launch an order and expect the supplier to have infinite inventory.

This concept is just as true whether we mail the supplier an order or send it to the supplier electronically.

JIT

Both MRP and DRP provide JIT needs when they are operated at zero safety time setting. Some people really believe that JIT means getting your supplier to carry your inventory. This concept is a short-term joke. Suppliers who are forced to carry inventory for their customer will eventually raise prices for that customer.

The only way that JIT will work on the long term with suppliers is as part of an MRP or DRP system that includes a contract with penalties for noncompliance for both sides. Nicey-nicey deals made on the golf course only last a couple of weeks at most.

Objectives

The objectives of both MRP and DRP are improved inventory management, for example (see illustration on page 155):

Give that team a raise. Give them the corporate quality award. They are making things happen. They are improving the quality of life in the company. They are making the company stronger for the future.

We find most companies do not measure performance this way. They look at the procedures—is the forecast accurate, are the inventory records accurate, are our people educated, are we professional, is this year's profit higher than last year's, are our earnings per share up, is our volume variance down, are the xerox expenses up, etc. etc.

The name of the game in business is return on investment and market share. Everything else is short-term Monopoly money. Customer service, lines worked, gross profit, and return on inventory are

154

Measures of Inventory Management Effectiveness
August xxxx

	This Year	Last Year
Customer Service	92.5%	90.3%
Turnover	4.6	4.3
Lines Worked	1,542,362	1,634,345
Gross profit	$ 12,030,456	$11,434,282
Average Inventory	$ 10,000,000	$ 10,000,000
GMROI	1.20	1.14

inventory management contributions to the company goals of return on investment and market share.

Focus Forecasting, MRP, and DRP all have these inventory management objectives as a fundamental driver.

Chapter 19 shows an action plan pilot to get going on DRP and Focus Forecasting for your company. It draws on case histories for its material. It's a proven path to fast results. You find out right away if your company is ready for paperless inventory management or if it's just lip service.

Some Thoughts on Current Practice

Over my years of managing inventory, there have come up a lot of practices that may or may not be sound. Here are some opposing viewpoints.

Consuming the Forecast

Consuming the forecast means keeping the total forecast for the month the same no matter what happens week by week as the month proceeds. This procedure was created on a lightning-filled night in an old English castle by a master planner who was tired of being jerked around by the real world. He reasoned as follows:

1. Forecast for March: 100 units, or 25 units per week
2. After one week if
   a. 25 were sold then the balance would be 25 25 25
   b. 50 were sold then the balance would be 0 25 25
   c. 0 were sold then the balance would be 50 25 25

Unfortunately, he created a monster. After all, if 50 were sold the first week in March (25 more than the forecast rate), would it not be more likely that more than 25 a week would be sold in the remaining weeks of March?

If 0 were sold the first week in March, would it not be more likely that fewer would be sold in the remaining weeks in March?

Worse yet, what would he do if 125 were sold the first week in March? Would he forecast that 25 would be returned in the remainder of the month?

Stop consuming the forecast. It will give you indigestion. Instead, don't give forecasts to MRP anymore. Let DRP match the forecast (Gross Requirements) against the current Master Production Schedule

156

(firm-planned orders). Let DRP critique the Master Production Schedule for suggested move-ups, move-backs, and cancels based on customer service and turnover needs.

Use rules that make sense for the critique. When you set your furnace thermometer at seventy degrees the furnace doesn't turn on until it is sixty-eight degrees and it doesn't turn off until it is seventy-five degrees. Set the action message parameters so you only suggest speedups when you will run out of stock if you don't speed up. Set the action message parameters so you only delay or cancel when you are creating excesses that are twice the lead time at least.

Once you have a good system for critiquing the Master Production Schedule, use DRP to do some rough-cut capacity planning. You can feed MRP the schedule rather than the forecast. As soon as you start driving MRP with a master schedule instead of raw forecast, you no longer need consume forecasts to keep from jumping around during the month. And better still, you won't have to explain to anybody what consuming the forecast is.

Available to Promise

When I was in charge of inventory at American Hardware, Customer Service wanted me to put delivery dates on customer orders we could not ship because we were out of stock. I refused to do so because if I had had enough precision to give a delivery date on an out-of-stock I would have been in stock in the first place.

Customer Service and MIS got together and married our expediting reports to our order entry system to automatically tell our customers when they would receive out-of-stock merchandise. It didn't work.

When our customers called me about our failure to honor the delivery date on the customer order I told them that MIS had created an automatic lie machine. If you purchase or produce to stock it is ten times better to work on being in stock in the first place than to develop automated systems to lie about future delivery dates.

Some companies make or purchase for individual orders or are in an environment where they accept orders inside the replenishment lead time only up to what they have already purchased or are in the process of making. In those companies, using available-to-promise logic makes sense. In those cases, DRP can show available-to-promise by distribution center for the purpose of accepting customer orders or quoting expected delivery on customer order inside the make or purchase lead time.

Safety Time

Safety time is the minimum weeks or days of supply in terms of future forecast that DRP will allow for an item.

I think calculating the inventory level needed to support a given service level by using probability tables and forecast error is hogwash.

Don't set safety time levels by using degree of forecast error. Most of the forecast error occurs in the worst-selling items in the company. Most of the excess inventory occurs in the worst-selling items in the company. When consultants learned this fact from actually using this procedure in companies, they tried to fix their error by suggesting using higher customer service goals (more multiples of forecast error) for the best-sellers and lower multiples for the worst-sellers. The fundamental concept is wrong in the first place.

Safety time covers at least thirty other problems in the inventory management equation other than forecast error. I've listed those other problems in chapter 11.

Half of all forecast error is where the forecast was higher than the actual. Why would anybody in his right mind want to carry more safety time on items whose forecast was high in the first place? And yet formulas for setting safety time based on forecast error ignore whether the forecast error was high or low.

The worst-sellers in the company have the most forecast error. By definition, when a company replenishes a worst-seller they automatically add safety time even when safety time is set to zero:

The replenishment ship pack is six and the safety time is zero for both items shown below:

Item A sells 100 per week.
Item C sells 6 per year.

On a weekly replenishment cycle the average inventory for each item is:

Item A: 50 pieces or 50/5200 = .01 year's supply
Item C: 3 pieces or 3/6 = .50 year's supply

Item C with a zero safety time setting averaged six months' safety time for the year. Why compound the problem by adding even more safety time by using forecast error to decide how much safety time to assign an item?

Safety Time and Review Time

It takes a certain amount of work to review an item, to order some for replenishment, to receive it into a warehouse, to put it on a shelf, to update the inventory records, to keep track of the on-order, and to pay the bills. It makes sense to review as infrequently as possible to keep down these operating costs.

The less frequently we review an item, however, the more inventory we carry. Take a look at this example:

**Average Inventory with
Review Frequency per Year**

	Annual Sales	52	26	12	6	1
Item A	5200	50	100	216	432	2600
Item B	6	1	1	1	1	3

It takes about the same amount of work to review item A or item B. So obviously we should review A much more frequently than B. Probably we order a year's supply of B whenever we order whether we like it or not, because B is packed six in a box.

Here's a sample rule for safety time and review time for:

	Volume		
	Items	Units	Dollars
A Items Heavy-traffic Items	5%	55%	33%
B Items Moderate-traffic Items	15%	25%	33%
C Items Slow-movers	80%	20%	33%

	Review Time Wks	Safety Time Wks	Inv Time Wks
A Items	1.0	3.0	3.5
B Items	8.0	1.0	5.0
C Items	13.0	0.0	6.5
Average			5.0

This strategy minimizes company units of work while putting the heaviest safety time in the best-sellers in the company. It is a lot easier to explain to a customer why you are out of pork rind ripple than to explain why you are out of vanilla. If you have an excess inventory it is a lot easier to sell off the vanilla.

Safety Stock

Safety stock is the minimum level of inventory that DRP will allow an item to run down to in future weeks.

The concept of safety time has almost made the concept of safety stock obsolete. It makes more sense to set a safety time at 3.0 weeks and have your DRP system dynamically adjust levels based on the season of the year coming up. Safety time increases snow shovel inventories in advance of winter sales and runs them down as spring arrives. Safety stock holds the same quantity regardless of future expected sales.

Safety stock is of value to make sure that the company has a minimum inventory without regard to the item's sales or usage volume. There are times when this concept is of value:

1. The company markets a critical drug or medicine that is seldom required but when it is required it is life-or-death.
2. The company has guaranteed a key customer that at least one pallet of this product will always be in stock.
3. A retail store needs a minimum number of boxes of diapers to fill the aisle space slots.

DRP uses the greater amount of safety time or safety stock. Most companies use only safety time because of the reduced need for file maintenance.

Lead Time

Lead time is the amount of time that passes from the time a buyer or planner reviews an item until it is on the shelf. The old reorder point concept of lead time was the average time it has taken in the past. The new DRP lead time concept is the negotiated lead time the supplier and the customer agree on as a consistent delivery period.

There is a lot of effort going into shortening lead time cycles in order to be able to react to changes in the marketplace. The shorter the lead time, the lower the commitment a customer has to make on purchase orders or factory orders. This is a good concept if it is coupled with DRP to show the supplier what is needed in the future and when it is needed. It is a good concept if procedures are changed to reduce work station and common carrier backlogs. It's a terrible concept if it only works a percentage of the time, putting most orders into expedite and special freight condition.

Short lead time is good. Consistent lead time is better. If orders arrive early sometimes and late sometimes there is a double dose of excess inventory. Companies must carry extra safety stock to cover late shipments. Companies will have excess inventories when goods arrive earlier than average lead time. Generally, companies have not paid for goods on order that have not been received. Longer lead times for the most part only mean more goods will be on order, not on hand.

A customer should negotiate lead time with a supplier, whether it is an outside supplier or an inside plant. The lead time should be the shortest consistent lead time from the supplier, not the best lead time the supplier has ever achieved. The issue is that the supplier must not ship early. Early shipments are overstocks for the customer. The supplier must not ship late. Late shipments are potential out-of-stocks for the customer. The major value of lead time is consistency, not how short it is.

Ship Packs

Plants and suppliers want to ship full pallets. Inventory managers would like to replenish in units of one piece. Whenever a company revises its current order quantity size it should evaluate the impact on the total inventory and lines of work.

In *Focus Forecasting: Computer Techniques for Inventory Control* there is a chapter devoted to new concepts of economic order quantity that do not require estimates of inventory carrying costs or inventory ordering costs.

Many companies will make up rules for order quantities that sound quite reasonable on the surface.

1. We will order six months' supply on items where the unit cost is less than two cents apiece.
2. We will always order in container loads, since our retail pricing requires the best cost of goods sold for us to be in the business.
3. This product is difficult to move, so it will always be palletized.
4. The supplier has a twenty-five-dollar start-up cost every time we order an XYZ, so we will order a year's supply at a time.

DRP can show the projected inventory level with the original policy and with the new policy. Then someone can ask management, "Is is worth x millions of dollars of inventory to always palletize bottled Malathion?"

162

Many times rules for minimum ship packs or minimum plant runs do more to ruin inventory turnover and consume scarce capacity than even the most horrendous forecasting system.

Transfers

Some companies abuse pegging. Pegging shows the on hand and the future planned orders for the distribution centers in the network. Some companies try to never buy or produce more inventory for the company if they can get away with transferring goods between distribution centers instead.

Generally speaking, it is not a good idea to make transfers to reduce ordering or producing more inventory. The work it takes checking every center for an imbalance outweighs the inventory saved by making the transfer.

Distribution centers don't like to make transfers to other distribution centers. Distribution centers have their own priority. It goes like this:

1. Ship customer orders. When distribution center sales go up, costs of operation as a percentage of sales go down.
2. Unload common carriers. Generally speaking, if the distribution center does not unload common carriers there will be a demurrage charge or at least a fight with the owner/driver.
3. Clear enough space off the receiving dock to continue to unload common carriers.
4. Sweep the floor and keep the warehouse spic-and-span for visiting customers and top management. Top management always rates the warehouse manager on how clean the warehouse is.
5. Have OSHA and Quality Circle meetings.
6. Transfer goods to other distribution centers if somebody complains. Sometimes the distribution center sees goods they have originally transferred to Texas coming back on a transfer to them. So if they wait long enough maybe the transfer will be canceled anyway.

I remember Customer Service asked me to make an exception to my rule not to initiate transfers to head off a customer out of stock on some breeze boxes during an unusually bad hot spell one summer. I said, "Just ship the goods direct from the other center to the customer." But Customer Service did not want to use a common carrier. They wanted to ship on our truck. They secretly made a deal to have the breeze boxes put on the tailgate of one of our trailers to go from one warehouse to the other. By the time the breeze boxes arrived the heat spell had broken and the customer canceled the order. The breeze boxes would have sold out in the original warehouse, but now they were excess inventory we would carry all winter.

Once every two or three months analyze the excess inventories by branch and make economical truckload balancing shipments between branches. Do it infrequently and with a well-informed branch manager. These transfers will be made on a timely basis and will reduce ordering in future periods. Transfer to reduce excess, not to head off customer out-of-stocks or to reduce today's ordering from the plant or supplier.

Dating

Dating is the practice some suppliers have of allowing companies to receive and use inventory and not pay for it until sometime in the future. Dating terms include 90 days, 120 days, and even 6 months.

Some buyers think that if they get dating on a purchase order they really have no inventory investment. Not true. The inventory risk is still there. The inventory handling and storage costs are still there. Dating is actually interchangeable with discounts. The value of 90 days' dating when money cost 12 percent is 1 percent a month, or about 3 percent.

Return on Inventory

If it was our money, then return on inventory would count a lot more than it does in companies today. Take two companies. Here is their performance:

	Company	
	A	**B**
Sales	$1,000,000	$1,000,000
Profit	200,000	200,000
Inventory	400,000	800,000
Return on Inventory	50%	25%

If those companies were banks, there is no question which company we would invest in. For every dollar we put in company A we'll earn fifty cents. For every dollar we put in company B we'll earn only twenty-five cents. That's not as absurd as it sounds. In most companies the inventory ranges from 50 percent to 150 percent of owners' equity.

Most companies, however, ignore return on inventory in their measures of top management performance. Here's a test. Your company reviews for ordering once a week, and you usually buy a month's supply. Your supplier comes in and offers you six months' dating and an extra ten to buy six months' supply. Just about every company I know would take the deal. It doesn't matter whether the goods in question are raw materials or goods for resale. But it's a bad deal. If it was our money we wouldn't do it. Here's why:

	Ordering a Month's Supply	Ordering a Six Month's Supply
Annual Sales	$12,000	$12,000
Cost of Goods	6,000	5,040
Gross Profit	6,000	6,960
Average Inventory	500	3,000
Return on Inventory	1200%	232%

165

Terrific deal that is. We are already making almost six times the return on inventory by not taking the deal. Unfortunately, company top management is usually measured on the short-term profit and loss statement and earnings per share. Eventually if they make enough poor trade-offs for more profit at the expense of return on inventory they usually go out of business. Test your company's gross profit return on inventory. If it is less than 100 percent you probably should be looking for a new job.

We have a chart, if you would like it, showing how much additional supply you should buy in exchange for each percentage point of added discount.

The next chapter shows a pilot action plan to actually start to change the way your company manages inventory.

PART IV

Chapter Nineteen

A Pilot Action Plan

The Pilot

I had been vice president of inventory control at American Hardware for twelve years before I started to think seriously of DRP. The reorder point system hooked up to Focus Forecasting was giving us good customer service and adequate inventory turnover. But there were some problems:

1. Home Depot, Houseworks, and some other giants were getting into the do-it-yourself market, putting pressure on us to promote and add new items to our inventory.
2. We were constantly promoting goods at off price and eventually had increased the number of items in our inventory by ten thousand items.
3. As we lowered prices and reduced our average volume per item we were pressed for cash, which in turn demanded that we achieve higher turnover.
4. We never could tell our warehouses what they might expect to receive in upcoming months with the reorder point system.
5. More and more we were making big buys to use as specials in national advertising. With our reorder point systems it was hard to buy the right mix of goods out into the future.

All of these things prompted me to bring in Andre Martin of Oliver Wight Associates to talk about DRP.

To tell the truth, I was apprehensive about switching over my entire inventory management to DRP. I was one of eight corporate officers making six figures and getting five weeks' vacation. I knew sometimes when a company totally resystematized an area when all was said and done there was a new organization to go with that system at the end. I might not come out on top.

We finally agreed to do a pilot on DRP to measure what the results might be and to learn more about how this new technology would impact me and American Hardware.

The results for the seven vendors in the pilot were extraordinary:

1. A 44 percent sales increase
2. A 25 percent gross profit increase
3. A 15 percent inventory reduction

In 1986 I started B.T. Smith and Associates. Ever since, when my son Chris and I work with clients our approach has been to start with a pilot program big enough so the benefits are worth the effort but not so big as to jeopardize the company if they fail. We rent the software to the company for the pilot project.

Some companies do not possess the strength to change the way they traditionally do things. It's better to find this out in a pilot program than in the throes of a major conversion.

When I was a corporate officer our young managers would come to us for approval of a project. Nothing was more impressive and persuasive to us than to see that they had already achieved some results without major investment. So usually the first step in any action plan we are involved in is to run a pilot program to train the participants and to demonstrate results.

An Action Plan for the Pilot

Here's an action plan to improve inventory management in your company in a selected area.

To: Management
Fr: The task force

XYZ Company Pilot
Inventory Management Action Plan

Objective: Evaluate the impact of using Focus Forecasting and DRP on:

1. Customer service
2. Turnover
3. Gross profit
4. Work

in the XYZ marketing and inventory management of goods supplied through Allentown, Atlanta, Columbus, Los Angeles, Seattle, and Hillsborough from the Seymour, IN plant.

Procedure: Use Focus Forecasting and DRP on a rental basis to manage forecasting, deployment, joint replenishment, excess inventory analysis, and master Production Schedule critique for all of the items in each of the warehouses produced by Seymour both aftermarket and EOM.

We have a task force made up of a person from each of the following areas:

1. Deployment
2. Plant
3. Marketing
4. Management Information Systems

Who	What	When
Task	1. Select a project team leader to handle all communications between B. T. Smith and the company.	Done
Task force	2. Visit and call on the phone companies already using Focus Forecasting and DRP.	
Team leader	3. Get approval from management for the pilot program	

171

Task force	4. Have a technical session with B. T. Smith to go over the necessary data elements needed by Focus Forecasting and DRP.
Task force	5. Purchase a modem and communications software to send and receive files from B. T. Smith.
Task force	6. Rent Focus Forecasting and DRP software.
MIS	7. Write programs to bring plant, warehouse, item, on-hand, demand history, and schedule receipt information to the Focus Forecasting and DRP systems.
B. T. Smith	8. Train operators in the initial use of the software.
Task force	9. Measure results with internal reports and with DRP 12 period summaries.
Task	10. Report results to management and detail recommendations for task force future development.

From the pilot program a company can put together a solid action plan to train the people in the company and to streamline use of the inventory management systems. Oliver Wight Associates, for example, has excellent educational courses, videotapes, class A audit procedures, proven path implementation procedures, and general know-how. B. T. Smith and Associates offers top management briefings and in-house education. APICS and the Council of Logistics Management have superb educational programs.

The arguments for leaping directly into a pilot program without major feasibility study and education are as follows:

1. People don't like to take risks. Many companies educate ad nauseam without ever actually doing anything to improve service or turnover. It's risk-free to sit in class and hear entertaining speakers. The rubber meets the road when you have to actually do something.

2. Nothing teaches like doing. About two thirds of the problem is knowing the right question to ask. Classes become more vitally interesting when a client must know the best answer to survive.
3. There is a lot of conceptual misinformation running rampant, in my opinion. It's theoretical stuff that doesn't do anything but employ consultants. Here's a laboratory to find out what's of real value and what's not.
4. The old mainframe systems were like pouring concrete. Once done it took an act of Congress to change them. Purchased systems cost six and seven figures. In those days it made sense to turn over every rock before doing anything. Not anymore.

The new way we suggest is to jump in with both feet. Get a pilot program running to find out the right questions to ask. It's impossible to sit down and imagine the 1 million branches on your inventory management tree in advance of starting. Many of the problems the company works on are not worth a hill of beans toward solving the real inventory management problems. Just putting together the data for a pilot program asks more of the right questions than a month of brainstorming.

Avoid paralysis by analysis. If you believe in any of the principles in this book, start using them before you lose them. Following are some case studies from successful Focus Forecasting and DRP users in their own words.

May this book be something of value for you and your company.

APPENDIXES

Appendix One

Contel Material Management: Fred Tolbert, Inventory Planning Manager

Introduction

CMMC is the procurement and distribution division of Contel Corporation, a $3 billion telecommunications company. It purchases, warehouses and distributes telecommunications products to the many operating divisions of its parent company. CMMC stocks four thousand products in four major distribution centers spread geographically across the country.

Two years ago, CMMC found itself with all of the textbook inventory problems. Namely, they had too much of the *wrong* product in the *wrong* place at the *wrong* time. The major symptoms of inventory problems surfaced in the areas of:

- Low customer service rate
- High inventory
- Lower productivity due to excessive order expediting
- High freight and procurement costs
- Poor relationships

Mainframe versus PC Strategy

As many companies do, CMMC primarily blamed "the system" for its inventory management problems. The company formed an informal project team to evaluate mainframe forecasting and DRP systems to integrate into the company's existing mainframe Distribution Management System. The group evaluated several of the major mainframe-based forecasting and DRP systems and made a preliminary selection. A cost/benefit study even suggested that the potential inventory reductions justified a mainframe-based system. However, the CMMC Management Advisory Committee, which approves major systems projects, rejected the project proposal. The major drawbacks to the mainframe strategy were cited as:

Money. The projected cost of the mainframe system, including software, hardware, additional manpower, and training, was estimated to be five hundred thousand dollars plus over a three-year period. That was more than upper management was willing to commit to any new system project.

Time. The mainframe system would require data-processing resources to be committed for a year or more. Little enthusiasm was generated for a system that would not begin a payback for at least twelve to eighteen months.

Risk. Major systems projects are never easy, especially one attempting to integrate mainframe packages from two different software companies. The preferred DRP software company claimed that the integration could be done, though they did not have experience making their system "talk" to our mainframe system. The technical risk associated with the mainframe approach was just too great.

The combination of money, time, and risk was more than the CMMC's top management was willing to gamble. The project team was instructed to find a less expensive and more effective alternative.

CMMC enlisted the assistance of a consultant to find alternative courses of action to improve inventory management performance. His recommendation was to utilize a personal computer–based DRP package to orient the company with the basic concepts of requirements planning. He recommended the use of Focus Forecasting and DRP microsoftware.

The consultant supported a pilot project implementation approach. This approach works by beginning DRP processing for one small product line, showing performance improvements, and then phasing in the other product lines. CMMC accepted the recommendation and chose one of its product lines to begin a DRP pilot. At the conclusion of the six-month DRP pilot project, CMMC began adding other major product lines to the Focus Forecasting and DRP system. By the end of the eighth month, CMMC was planning over 90 percent of its on-hand inventory utilizing Focus Forecasting and DRP.

Major Advantages of the PC Approach

Looking back on the DRP project, CMMC management cited the following advantages to the PC implementation approach:

- *Low risk/low cost.* The PC approach allowed the company to convert from a reorder point system to a requirements planning environment with a minimal investment in software and computer hardware. The technical data-processing environment required to download data from the existing mainframe system to the PC is relatively simple, allowing a low-risk implementation.
- *Lower MIS effort.* The PC approach requires much less MIS department programming support compared to the typical mainframe-based system.
- *Hands-on education and training.* CMMC users received hands-on DRP education and software training within days of acquiring the PC software. Users learned the new DRP inventory-planning concepts by interacting with "live" data that they work with every day. The pilot approach provided users with a less threatening environment in which to learn the new inventory management concepts.
- *Realize DRP benefits immediately.* The pilot approach method allowed the company to begin achieving improvements in customer service and inventory turnover soon after beginning the DRP project.
- *Smooth transition to future mainframe system.* CMMC's strategic plans include developing a full integrated, corporate-wide logistics system. Having learned DRP operations in a low risk/low cost environment will pay dividends later during the hectic mainframe implementation.

Project Performance Measures

DRP is designed to improve the four key success measures of a distribution company. Therefore, improvements in these measures should be the goals of the implementation project.

Below are the four key success measures of DRP success, followed by CMMC's documented results following one year on the DRP system:

- *Goal 1 = > Higher Customer Service.* CMMC monitors its sales order line fill rate on a daily basis. This measure has improved from 82 percent at the beginning of the project to a current level of 93.5 percent.
- *Goal 2 = > Higher Inventory Turnover.* CMMC monitors inventory turnover, by product line, on a monthly basis. With DRP, inventory turns have stabilized in the 5.0 to 6.0 range. CMMC is also beginning to stock more low-demand items, in response to its customers' higher line fill expectations. These new items have had an impact on the company inventory turn number. The company recently set a new, aggressive target of improving turns to the 7 + turns level.
- *Goal 3 = > Higher Gross Margin.* Improved customer service and better supplier relations lead to increased sales and gross margin dollars. To facilitate these improvements, many companies work directly with suppliers to provide them with DRP planning schedules in exchange for additional discounts and firm lead times. CMMC is currently initiating this process, known as supplier scheduling, as part of its overall supplier negotiation strategy. It expects to see improvements in pricing, on-time supplier delivery, and reduced lead times as a result.
- *Goal 4 = > Higher productivity.* One key productivity measure that CMMC uses is the number of customer backorder lines requiring expediting. As the line fill rate has steadily increased, the number of backorder lines requiring expediting has fallen by 50 percent.

Major Lessons Learned

CMMC learned many lessons during its Focus Forecasting and DRP implementation. Among the major lessons learned were:

180

- *Involve line management.* The DRP project "Rambos" did not have organizational responsibility for inventory turnover and customer service. During the early phases of the project, the line managers who did have inventory management responsibility did not completely buy-in to the new system. The conflicts between those line and staff functions delayed CMMC achieving the benefits of the new system. Line management must take ownership in the new system for it to be successful.
- *Lack of consistent operating procedures.* CMMC found that as many stockouts were caused by not adhering to system-operating procedures as from forecast error and supplier deliveries. Among the procedures that must be strictly adhered to are: 1) Weekly DRP review of all product lines; 2) Working all DRP action messages, including expedite and de-expedite action messages; and 3) Periodic item analysis, which includes maintaining accurate item lead times, safety stock parameters, and standard pack size data.
- *System overrides.* CMMC inventory planners and Forecast Analysis frequently overrode the system because the numbers "didn't look right." Eventually we developed a rule to only override the system when you know something that the system does not.
- *Concentrating on customer service at the expense of inventory turns.* CMMC made dramatic improvements in its measure of customer service, line fill rate. However, during that time, total inventory increased by over 34 percent. The company concentrated so hard on its line fill rate that it sacrificed inventory turns. When total inventory reached an all-time high, a major program to improve inventory turns was initiated.
- *Managing supplier lead times.* CMMC traditionally accepted the fact that supplier lead times were unpredictable. After a year and a half of DRP operations, they began measuring their supplier's delivery performance. The first supplier to be measured was providing on-time deliveries only 18 percent of the time. CMMC should have begun concentrating on supplier deliveries much sooner in its DRP implementation project.

Conclusion

CMMC learned that there are alternatives to initiating mainframe-based software projects. The processing power contained in the new generation of PCs, coupled with the availability of Focus Forecasting and DRP microsoftware, makes a PC-based implementation attractive. The PC approach provided CMMC with the benefits of a mainframe-based system while significantly reducing the money, time, and risk associated with major software projects.

Ultimately, people determine the success or failure of a DRP project. DRP is a tool that helps people improve the four success measures of a distribution performance. CMMC found that PC-based DRP was the right way to go!

Appendix Two

Avery International: Jim Seafort, Corporate Consultant

K & M's Solution to Improved Inventory Management

The problem was to develop systems, policies, and procedures to improve inventory management at K&M Company, a division of Avery. As manufacturing consultant at Avery's corporate offices, I was given this assignment in mid-1989 with the objective of producing results within one year.

K&M is a market leader in the manufacture of notebooks, sheet protectors, and communication boards. The company has two manufacturing sites in Southern California and five remote distribution centers spread throughout the United States. We stock over two thousand skus at each distribution center, shipping approximately five thousand orders to customers each day.

In the past two to three years, K&M experienced dramatic sales growth, centered primarily in the Midwest and East. During this time, efficient management of finished goods and the coordination of customer demands back to the manufacturing plant for procurement and assembly had deteriorated significantly. By 1989, inventory turns were down to less than 4.0—unacceptable for high-volume, repetitive business.

K&M needed a fast, simple solution to its inventory/distribution turnover problem. Since we had neither the time nor the budget to revamp our entire mainframe system, we required a niche solution that would accurately forecast customer demand at each distribution center, ensure that inventory was deployed on a timely basis, and create a master schedule for our two manufacturing plants.

To achieve these objectives, we selected the PC solutions from Focus Forecasting and DRP from B. T. Smith and Associates. We were looking for down-to-earth inventory management professionals who could provide us with experience and support as well as effective, flexible software.

We began by retrieving accurate historical sales data for each distribution center. We reviewed each order and used only actual customer shipments in the data base, eliminating inventory transfers between distribution centers. Although we were able to obtain only twelve months of sales history, Focus Forecasting generated a reasonably accurate forecast without using the program's seasonality feature.

At the same time, we developed a decision table for globally setting inventory policies of safety stock and lot size for our five distribution centers. Each parameter conforms to days of forecast, not fixed quantities. This allows for safety stock and lot sizes to increase when sales are heavy and decrease when sales are low. Then, using the standard formula to calculate average inventory (safety stock plus one-half lot size), we were able to predict what our inventory investment would be based on our inventory policy table.

An example of K&M's inventory policy table is shown below to demonstrate how the forecasting works.

ABC Class Code	Safety Stock	Lot Size
A Items	2.0 Weeks	2.0 Weeks
B Items	3.0 Weeks	3.0 Weeks
C Items	6.0 Weeks	8.0 Weeks

We installed the integrated Focus Forecasting and DRP systems with our mainframe (MRP) in January 1990. Training commenced immediately and was completed within one month. Results have been outstanding. Three months after integration, our purchasing and planning departments were able to improve raw materials' turns from 6.4 to 14.4. After six months of use, we improved overall inventory turns from 3.6 to 5.8.

The DRP system also contributed two unique applications to the K&M operations. While running DRP and utilizing the "bill of material" processing feature, we have been able to generate rough-cut capacity plans, routing instructions, and labor requirements. DRP output produces a capacity plan for each work center. Each plan is also "pegged," so that we can determine which items to cut back to meet capacity constraints. We are also using DRP to help us determine scheduling. By consolidating all of our distribution center requirements into a "dummy" center, we can generate a combined, time-phased master schedule—which is also pegged. Updated requirements are loaded into our MRP mainframe on a weekly basis to ensure that the finished goods plan is in agreement with the raw materials plan, further supporting our improved raw material turns goal.

Based on the flexible and logical file structures in both the DRP and Focus Forecasting systems, we have found it quite easy to develop custom software to enhance the standard operating features of both programs. We recently added an inventory analysis module so that we could examine each part number in descending turns order, within each distribution center and within each ABC classification. By accessing this data, we can analyze slow-moving inventory and verify conformance to our inventory policies. This program takes only eight minutes to run, providing planners with easy access to critical information on our overall inventory position.

We are now confident we can increase overall turns to over 7.0 by the end of 1990, cutting our inventory by another 50 percent. To further improve our results, we plan to:

1. Network the software to customer service, production control, and each of the distribution centers.
2. Electronically launch work orders directly from the DRP system to the shop floor.
3. Strategically cut our lead times by one-half.

The management control we gained over inventory and distribution was accomplished with no additional staff or organizational changes. Those involved in the development and installation of the system secured critical mastery and ownership over their jobs and the inventory investment. We can now predict, with certainty, what our customer-service levels will be, based on our inventory policies. We have made inventory planners throughout the company responsible for the dollars of inventory, not just the units.

Something they never could have accomplished before.

Appendix Three

CXA Limited/ICI Explosives: Royden Brown, Demand Management Supervisor

ICI Explosives, with headquarters in Toronto, Ontario, Canada, is a worldwide manufacturer and distributor of explosives and related articles. CXA Limited is a business unit of ICI Explosives with two manufacturing sites in Canada. The products manufactured at these sites include initiation devices that are used throughout North America in the mining, construction, quarry, logging, and oil exploration industries. CXA's main manufacturing facility is located in Brownsburg, Quebec, with a secondary site in Tappen, British Columbia. The number of end products (skus) that are currently manufactured and sold to customers exceeds forty-five hundred items.

Some of these products are stocked at any of thirteen distributors located across Canada, from where the end customer receives the product.

In 1985 CXA made the decision to implement MRP II at its manufacturing facilities. Forecasting prior to implementation was limited to the yearly sales plan by product line. Production planning was basically a reorder point type system, with the sales and planning supervisors managing the order entry, factory scheduling, and customer service functions. Some of the measurements at that time showed that customer service, scheduling accuracy, inventory accuracy, etc., were in the mid 70 percent range. CXA installed an IBM System 38 and went with DATA 3 for the MRP software. Personnel at CXA took on an eager approach to fully implement MRP II and become Class A users and in fact reached that position in September 1988. The 1989 realized results gave measurements in the high 90 percent range for most key areas such as inventory, product structure, and scheduling accuracy.

The need of a forecasting package became evident during the implementation of MRP II. CXA, though, was not convinced how best to proceed, especially given the number of complex forecasting packages and mainframe software options. It was during the course of education for MRP that the Focus Forecasting concept came up as a very simple yet effective way to forecast. Unfortunately, it had been used on a mainframe and CXA did not wish to proceed with that type of installation. It was a short time later that Steve Johnston approached CXA with a microcomputer version of the same forecasting package. CXA evaluated the package, then realizing its potential, purchased it and thus became the third micro user of the software.

The use of Focus Forecasting at CXA initially started with manually keying in the sales volumes from the various subfamilies and families. Forecasting was performed following month end, and the marketing manager confirmed or adjusted the volumes that were presented to him. The resulting forecast volumes were then manually inputted into the MRP system and exploded down to a sku level through a forecast planning bill in the MRP system. Forecasting in this manner was used for over one year and was sufficient for many of the products that CXA manufactures. Many of the products, though, that CXA manufactures and sells have high seasonality associated with them, and this would not be recognized without making numerous changes to the planning bill percentages in the MRP system. It was decided that in order to take full advantage of Focus Forecasting the sales volume information at a sku level needed to be downloaded into Focus Forecasting to let the demand pattern of each individual product play more of a role in the aggregate forecast.

Currently on the Monday following a month end, the sales information for the month at a sku level is downloaded into an IBM Model 70. As a result of new product introductions and conversions, as well as private labeling arrangements, the number of products currently in the forecast data base is in the neighborhood of forty-five hundred items. Under normal circumstances a batch forecast is done overnight. During the following two days adjustments are made at a sku level, a filter program is run to highlight unusual demand, and aggregation by family is performed. The totals for volume and dollars by product family for the next twelve months are presented to marketing for final approval. The family total volumes are inputted into sales and operation planning sheets for discussion at the monthly Business Plan meeting on Thursday, During Friday forecast analysis programs are run and any fine-tuning of the forecast is done, with the end result being that the forecast by end product is uploaded electronically for the MRP run on the weekend.

While the results indicated that the forecasting had improved, CXA was still experiencing unusual demand patterns in the short term because of inventory control practices by distributors who order and own their inventory. It was suggested to the marketing manager, Morris Bannerman, by CXA's MRP consultant, Andre Martin, that there existed an opportunity to investigate a DRP link. Distributors would use DRP and send their planned orders to CXA by product on a weekly basis. CXA by receiving this time-phased information would be in a better position to produce material that was needed at the correct time. As a consequence, the distributor as well would be able to reduce inventories, knowing they would receive their planned orders.

In the spring of 1987 two distributor managers agreed to participate in a pilot program. The managers and their inventory control personnel were educated in DRP concepts and principles by Bernie Smith and myself acting as project coordinator for the pilot program. The distributors at the time were managing inventory on a reorder point type system within the microcomputer-based accounting software in use at each location. Software links to download the relevant information such as on-hand balances, lead times, safety times, case quantities, etc., into the DRP software were developed by B. T. Smith and Associates. The planning horizon for all products was set at thirteen weeks. The inventory control personnel at each location on a weekly basis went through a procedure in which the on-hand balances, open customer orders, forecasts, etc., were updated in the DRP software.

Planned orders generated by DRP were managed in the four-week period from the current date, with the distributor firming up the customer order two weeks prior to receiving it into their inventory. Problem products were highlighted to the distributor for possible action to either reschedule out any existing order or try to expedite product from CXA to eliminate a stockout. When the distributor finished working DRP for the week they would electronically transmit the planned orders by product as well as any firmed up customer orders to CXA via a modem-to-modem hookup with a microcomputer at CXA. Transmission time for the 400–450 items the distributor had worked was approximately ten minutes.

Meanwhile, at CXA the transmitted file is loaded into the DRP software and the distributor's product numbers are converted to CXA's part numbers. The planned orders for the next thirteen weeks as well as any firm customer orders from the distributor get electronically uploaded into the MPS. Material to match the planned orders is allocated against the customer number, thereby giving Production Planning visibility into future orders. Overnight an exception report is generated for any problem items that do not have sufficient quantities to meet the planned order demand. Customer service personnel first examine if production planning can accommodate any change, and second, if no change can be made then the distributor is informed that a possible problem exists in delivery for that product.

While the problem may very well be short-term, the distributor may be able to take alternative action, knowing they could be in a stockout situation for that particular product several weeks in the future. The distributors (customers) are happy that they were receiving an almost 100 percent order fill rate as well as the knowledge that when a potential problem exists they were able to take preventative measures. The distributor personnel see this as being very progressive to managing their inventories better.

Results from the pilot program have proven to be very positive, with order fill rate for the distributors increasing to 99 percent, inventory turns going upwards from 5 to 9, improved customer service, lower inventories, and in general less work associated with inventory management. The distributor was able to reduce many small orders being placed on CXA over a two-week period to one order being placed to replenish the inventory. At CXA the short-term (up to three months) forecast of total demand is replaced with a forecast for non-DRP customers and a consolidation of planned orders from DRP customers. The total demand for all customers is still generated using Focus Forecasting for months 4 through 12 and is uploaded into the MRP system for requirement planning. For CXA, Master Scheduler Robert Frappier says that his production planners are able to make better use of actual planned orders by producing product that is needed rather than producing material based on previous forecasts or simply for the replenishment of safety stocks.

The production planning department has reacted by putting more trust in the planned orders rather than producing according to an incorrect forecast.

For the future, ICI Explosives feels so positively with the gains that have been made with DRP that over the next twelve months it is committed to bring upward of 85 percent of the CXA's business to operate in this fashion with another ten distributor locations throughout Canada and the United States. As a manufacturer, CXA is committed to maintaining a high level of customer service while maintaining inventories at a reasonable level. It has been able to achieve this by planning based on the distributors' planned orders for the short term through the use of DRP while at the same time using Focus Forecasting for the medium- and longer-term horizon.

Appendix Four

Whirlpool Corporation: Bill Dunwoodie, Logistics Manager

Whirlpool is the world's largest appliance corporation, with over six billion dollars in sales annually.

LaPorte is the international aftermarket part and accessory distribution center for the Whirlpool Corporation.

Year after year LaPorte provided Whirlpool and Kenmore customers with tops in industry part availability. However, during the late eighties a combination of reorganizations, retirements, high turnover, and aging systems caused service level to slip. A team was put together in June of 1989 to find an immediate solution to improve customer service.

The team consisted of two information system analysts and two inventory control supervisors. The team started on a lengthy system requirements definition process. During the initial phase of the process it was evident the majority of the system user group were not aware of modern logistic technologies such as DRP, etc. It was determined the help of outside consultants was needed. The team went through the consultant selection process—first presenting the problems and then receiving the "standard" consultant pitch on how they would be solved. Their solutions were leading toward lengthy mainframe installation solutions. While going through this process the team discovered Bernie Smith's DRP/Focus Forecasting solution. The team selected the DRP/Focus Forecasting systems for the following reasons:

1. The system could be implemented in a short period of time compared to the other consultants' mainframe solutions—and customer service needed improvement immediately.

191

2. The cost of the system was minimal in comparison to that of a large mainframe system.
3. The aftermarket parts distribution business is a classic application of the Pareto principle (80/20 rule). We could put the high-activity parts in the DRP in a short period of time and bring the majority of the business back to acceptable customer-service levels.
4. We planned to continue pursuing a long-term mainframe solution while we were implementing Bernie Smith's DRP.
5. It would provide an immediate education on DRP and forecasting technologies.

It was determined the DRP would be implemented first and Focus Forecasting second. The DRP system was implemented in less than six months from date of purchase. The DRP system consisted of three modules:

1. *Forecasting module:* Define independent customer demand and determine what levels of packaged (finished) parts inventory are necessary to meet established service-level goals.
2. *Packaging module:* Translate finished inventory requirements into packaging facility production schedule.
3. *Purchasing module:* Determine that parts, accessories, and components are necessary where and when for packaging. Provide expedite/de-expedite messages to react to changes in customer demand.

Organizational Issues

The department was organized under the order point system with buyers, inventory control analysts, and expediters. The buyers negotiated pricing, established vendors, etc. The inventory analysts processed the order point purchasing messages, and the expediters performed the phone follow-up. It was determined with DRP the buyers would perform their traditional negotiation and pricing tasks and review DRP action messages. The job of the inventory analyst was eliminated. Expediters would continue to perform the phone follow-up if necessary.

After seven months of implementation experience it was determined the impact of DRP on individual job roles/department organization had been underestimated. A DRP organizational impact team consisting of a buyer, analyst, and expediter was put together to recommend an organization that effectively utilizes DRP. They recommended the buyer return to a vendor base management role—reduce vendor base, negotiate pricing, quality, etc. A new position of an inventory planner will review DRP action messages. The expediters will continue phone follow-up. Their recommendations are in the process of implementation.

Another area of organizational impact was the departmental product structure. Under order point the department was organized along the lines of product: laundry, refrigeration, etc. With DRP it was determined the department is organized by vendors. This allows a buyer to focus on all business with an individual vendor—not just the laundry or refrigeration business.

Performance Measurements

DRP implementation returned our service level on the high-activity parts to the 95 percent goal within four months.

Increased availability of the high-activity parts improves market share and increases sales and profits. The total dollar amount has yet to be determined.

Department morale has improved. Improved service level has reduced the level of stress from last year. Significantly less time is spent reacting to "fire drills."

Inventory initially increased on these parts; however, the projected turns have remained approximately the same. It was our intention to satisfy the customer needs first, then really focus on reducing inventories by reducing DRP safety times and improving forecasting accuracy with the implementation of Focus Forecasting.

Implementation Issues

I. Future Challenges

Implementation of DRP should be thought of as the start of a new era in logistics management, not the end of an old order point system. We still have to learn how to share DRP planned order information with both our customers and suppliers. This sharing of information should be done to increase profit, not because it is the next technology step.

Another challenge is getting the remaining parts into DRP. There is a definite productivity improvement in DRP versus order point. However, in order to put parts into DRP we have found it necessary to "clean up" the parts first. By cleaning up we mean determining the lead times are accurate and minimum order quantities are correct, etc.

II. Mistakes (Items You Would Have Done Differently If Given the Chance)

The people that use the system have to take ownership, or it is doomed to fail. At first just the DRP team made the decisions. The users would question us from day one. The system really started working once the users bought into it and started seeing changes they specifically wanted. A good example of this is the expediter report.

Training, Training, and More Training

It is difficult to keep a perspective on what the users know about the system. If part of the development team, you tend to take things for granted. Users have their day-to-day tasks to perform, and training will take the back burner—especially in times of crisis.

III. Strengths

The development team successfully combined experience and

knowledge of the old system with energy and enthusiasm and new technologies. The team consisted of:

Ralph Lemcke—twenty-five-plus years' of experience of LaPorte inventory management. Extensive knowledge of order point inventory management and the parts business.
Warren Wollert—twenty-plus years' experience in LaPorte systems. Extensive knowledge of the LaPorte computer systems.
Dave Hughes—new MIS analyst. Whiz kid with PCs and understanding new technologies.
Bill Dunwoodie—team leader, new inventory management supervisor. Logistics MBA with understanding of project management skills.

The team worked together well because everyone on the team played an important role and the skills complemented each other.

Summary

The new DRP system works. It has improved service level in a short period of time with minimal investment in software and hardware. DRP at LaPorte is at a new beginning—there is still a long way to go. Implementation of Focus Forecasting should only improve the system. What will be done for a long-term mainframe system has been put on hold. The mainframe acts only as a data base to hold information for PCs. We plan to continue putting parts into DRP.

Appendix Five

Ciba-Geigy: Sylvain Landry, Administrator, Systems and Accounting

The DRP implementation took place at the pharmaceuticals division of Ciba-Geigy Canada LTD, located in Dorval, Quebec.

Distribution Network

The distribution network consists of one consolidation center located in Dorval (plant site) and one distribution center in Calgary, Alberta.

Prior to the implementation of DRP, inventory management was based on a simple "number of days of supply" model. Transportation costs were high because of back-and-forth movements and numerous last-minute air shipments. The number of backorders in Calgary was higher than Dorval's, indicating that the inventory was often in the right quantities but in the wrong location.

Materials planning was based on MRP logic using national forecasts and national inventory levels (i.e., not taking into account the DC network). The system was a modified MAPICS software implemented in the early eighties that we called P.P.A.M.M.

DRP Project

The need for DRP was recognized in 1987. Since the whole question of MRPII and MRPII software was being debated with no specific timetable established, Materials Management was looking for a PC-based software that could be implemented quickly and improve service level. This software would take its information from current order entry and MRP systems through simple interfaces transferable to other systems if need existed.

The DRP software manufactured and distributed by B. T. Smith and Associates was the only product that met these requirements.

The project was organized into two distinct phases:

Phase I: The "downloading" of all the necessary information from order entry and MRP systems (e.g., item number, description, lot size, lead time, safety stock, forecasts, scheduled receipts, firm planned orders, etc.) in order to have DRP operational.

Phase II: The "uploading" of the DRP outputs (distribution orders, planned orders, etc.) into the master-scheduling function of P.P.A.M.M.

In short, phase I would permit the replacement of the "number of days of supply" model used to manage the inventory at the DC level. Even though the DRP software wouldn't be fully integrated with materials planning (P.P.A.M.M.), i.e., the planning function would still be performed based on national inventory levels, DRP could highlight potential supply problems and permit short-term manual adjustments at the master-scheduling level. We felt that the full integration (download and upload of the information) would take a lot of time and resources and preferred the two-phase approach.

Phase I was implemented in December 1988. The scope of this phase was kept within Materials Management and MIS. MIS was involved in writing interface programs between order entry, P.P.A.M.M., and DRP.

Historical ratios were used to break the national forecast between Dorval and Calgary (the same ratio was also used to split safety stock). DRP was also added to the monthly sales and operations-planning agenda to highlight possible events that might change this historical ratio.

We would like to recognize the contribution of the following people from Materials Management:

Sylvain Landry, Administrator, Systems and Accounting (who acted as the project coordinator)
Jean Lemay, Manager, Logistics
Gaetan Rouleau, Distribution Planner (to be DRP planner)
Louis M. Tessier, Director, Materials Management

and, from MIS,

Jocelyn Guimond, Director, Management Services (MIS)
Robert Lanoureux, Computer Analyst

Performance Results

In 1989 transportation costs to Calgary DC were reduced by 25 percent. The number of backorders were about equal at Calgary and Dorval, meaning that when backorders occurred they occurred nationally, i.e., it was not a case of having the inventory at the wrong location (keep in mind that the service level at Ciba-Geigy is about 99 percent with an inventory coverage relatively low for the industry).

The company recognized the benefits of DRP and decided to go ahead in 1990 with phase II. A project team was set up including members from Marketing, Sales, Materials Management, and MIS to establish a timetable. This project is presently underway.

Appendix Six

Fisher Controls: Mike A. Thomas, CPIM

Fisher Controls International Inc. is the leader in the manufacture of control valves and one of the leading manufacturers of Process Instrumentation.

The Austin, Texas facility is a staging site for Process Control Systems. The Leicester, England, facility manufactures the printed wire boards for all Fisher Staging locations and also serves as a staging site for Process Control Systems.

In 1989 a need was identified for Fisher, Austin, to significantly improve the process of transferring forecast information to our Leicester facility. The Austin site also had a requirement to provide more accurate information on Leicester products to the people who dated our customer orders. At that time it took six to twelve working days to generate the forecast using spread sheets, sending the spread sheets to Leicester via electronic mail and manually downloading the data to their Master Schedule. The process involved rekeying the forecast several times, which introduced data errors. This was compounded by the fact that Leicester had to repeat this process for three other sites. Because a new forecast was generated every month, for a significant part of each month, the two plants were operating on different production forecasts.

Since Fisher, Austin, was evaluating the purchase of a new manufacturing system and computer, the requirements that needed to be satisfied were:

- Cost-effective (not a lot of money involved)
- Easy implementation and interface to our current mainframe
- Improved ability to communicate both internally and externally

- Flexibility to interface the system to other manufacturing systems

Jon Leyen, Program Director CIM, researched available DRP software and allocated the money to purchase the B. T. Smith DRP package. Mary Robertson, Project Manager CIM, and Mike Thomas, Commodity Manager, were assigned to implement and run the new package.

When the software was initially implemented, we concentrated on improving our internal communications. The Austin forecast was downloaded to the DRP software. This was updated with the scheduled receipts from Leicester. The reports from the DRP system then provided accurate and timely information for dating orders. After this process was established we began to focus on the use of the DRP package for external communications. Additional copies of the DRP software were purchased for the Leicester site. We began implementing DRP as a multisite tool, with the following results:

- It now takes one to two days to produce the forecast, download to Leicester, and input to their master schedule. (This used to take six to twelve days.)
- We now have information on problem PWBs identified and requests sent to Leicester in one to two hours.
- A plan is in place to have all Fisher staging locations worldwide use DRP to provide PWB forecast to Leicester.
- A plan is in place to use DRP to transmit supply information from Leicester to the staging sites (Closed Loop).

We feel that the speed and accuracy of this type of communications will help establish Fisher Controls as the leader in Process Instrumentation.

Summary

Although we did not initially use the DRP package to its full potential, it became apparent what impact this "tool" could have on us. We still continue to improve communication between sites using the DRP software. The excellent support provided by B. T. Smith and Associates was a major factor in minimizing implementation problems. We are looking forward to tying DRP into our new mainframe.

Appendix Seven

Rohm and Haas: Guillermo L. Vernengo, Industrial Engineer Inventory Systems Analyst

A DRP Application at Rohm and Haas

The need for a better share of the market and customer service triggered a search for a better way to replenish stock levels at several branches. The traditional fixed order point routines plus the Min Max brought deficiencies in the system. Stockouts and complaints about deliveries were in abundance.

It did not take too much time to decide to switch to a better technique. Results of the traditional systems were showing.

The micro DRP software required a very simple installation in the PC. Rohm and Haas developed a system that made good use of the two worlds of computers: the records needed to run the DRP were developed at the mainframe level, where data resides and where it is easier to format the records using the SAS programming language; then the files are downloaded to the PC, where the DRP software does the number crunching at a higher speed and much lower cost. The user does that by typing a simple word command; a completion message tells what to do next.

The mechanization of the replenishment orders was not the only objective in mind; Rohm and Haas did not want to put every item in the product list as a "DRP item"; an ABC analysis helped in determining which skus were the best to be kept in stock and to be replenished as the DRP-recommended replenishment. The ABC analysis covered national as well as regional activity.

The transition between the old system and the DRP approach was very smooth indeed, and quick. Rohm and Haas has a forecasting system in place; forecasting by branch and region helped to meet the requirements of a DRP system where local demand generates local planned orders that are subsequently scheduled for manufacturing.

Soon after the skus were physically in place at the designated branch warehouses, the logic started to work; inventory levels went down and the DRP responded swiftly to the impact of a sudden rush of orders due to preannouncement of price increases or to the simple sales promotions. Quickly the system generated larger planned orders, followed by shipments arriving in the following weeks. In general, customer service went up and complaints due to stockouts stopped.

The system was designed so the maintenance of parameters and files was left to the users' needs. Actually, the user could create records, delete them, or modify parameters such as transit lead times, safety times, safety quantities, batch sizes, etc., at the mainframe level. As business conditions changed, the user adjusted parameters without affecting the data bases.

Later versions of microsoftware DRP helped the users when a stream of function keys' commands were put together in batch files.

In addition to the improvements in the critical areas of customer service and inventory reductions, the replenishment process became a smooth and disciplined procedure, and the paper shuffling that accompanied the old traditional system was eliminated.

These successes, the relatively rapid and smooth implementation, and the low cost of running the system prompted Rohm and Haas to extend the application of the distribution techniques to other locations and product lines.

Currently the company has covered five product lnes, including the entire manufacturing processes in two foreign subsidiaries where MRP has been added to the DRP.

Appendix Eight

Some Sample DRP Networks

A BREWING COMPANY

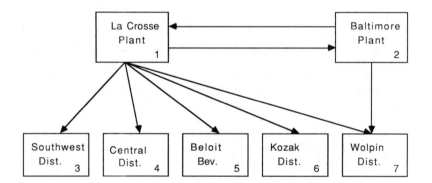

A COIL/SHEET MANUFACTURER

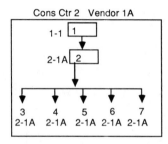

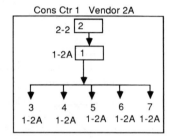

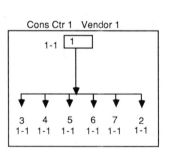

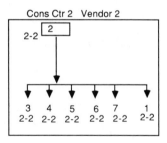

A DISTRIBUTOR OF PARTS

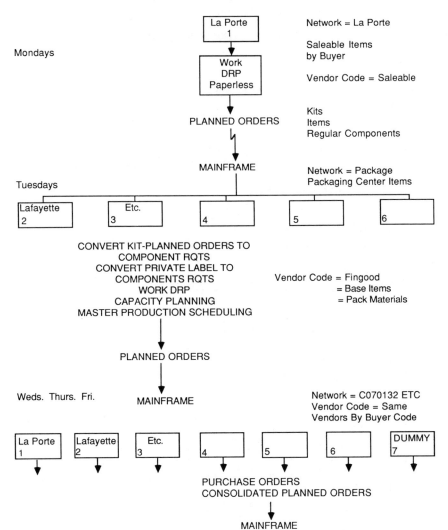

Mondays

La Porte
1

Work
DRP
Paperless

PLANNED ORDERS

MAINFRAME

Network = La Porte

Saleable Items
by Buyer

Vendor Code = Saleable

Kits
Items
Regular Components

Network = Package
Packaging Center Items

Tuesdays

| Lafayette 2 | Etc. 3 | 4 | 5 | 6 |

CONVERT KIT-PLANNED ORDERS TO
COMPONENT RQTS
CONVERT PRIVATE LABEL TO
COMPONENTS RQTS
WORK DRP
CAPACITY PLANNING
MASTER PRODUCTION SCHEDULING

Vendor Code = Fingood
= Base Items
= Pack Materials

PLANNED ORDERS

MAINFRAME

Weds. Thurs. Fri.

Network = C070132 ETC
Vendor Code = Same
Vendors By Buyer Code

| La Porte 1 | Lafayette 2 | Etc. 3 | 4 | 5 | 6 | DUMMY 7 |

PURCHASE ORDERS
CONSOLIDATED PLANNED ORDERS

MAINFRAME

207

A FOOD PROCESSOR

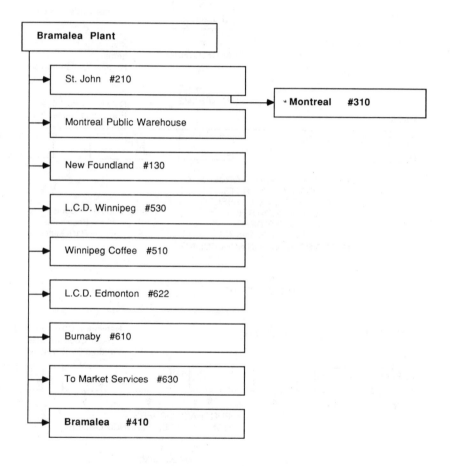

A HEAVY HARDWARE MANUFACTURER

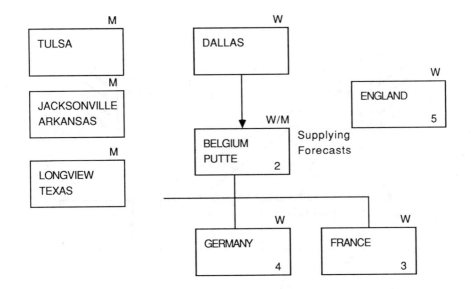

M

TULSA

M

JACKSONVILLE
ARKANSAS

M

LONGVIEW
TEXAS

W

DALLAS

W/M

BELGIUM
PUTTE   2

Supplying
Forecasts

W

ENGLAND
        5

W

GERMANY
        4

W

FRANCE
        3

A MANUFACTURER OF ANIMAL PRODUCTS

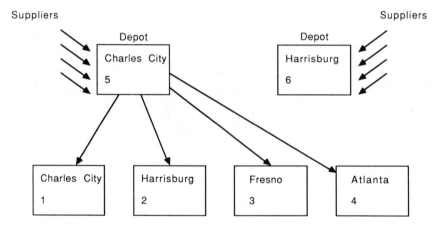

A MANUFACTURER OF CABINETS

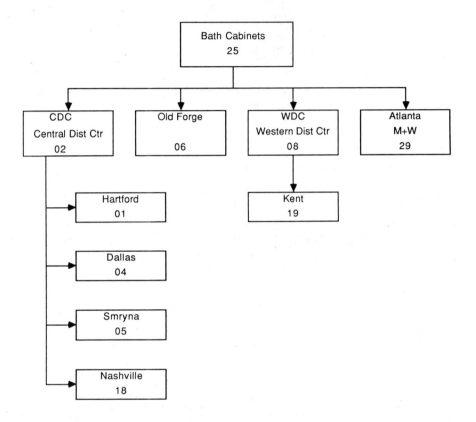

A MANUFACTURER OF CABINETS (CONT.)

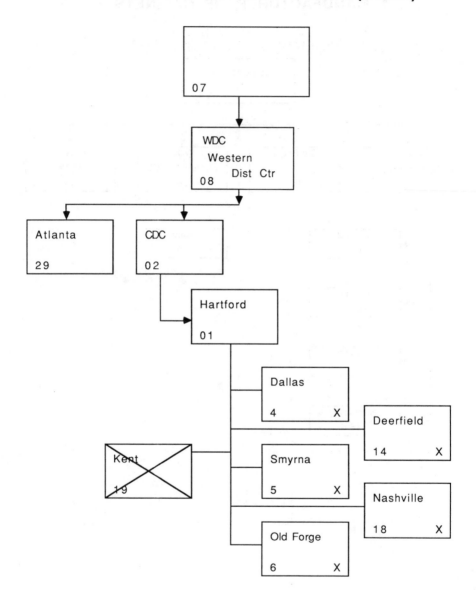

A MANUFACTURER OF CABINETS (CONT.)

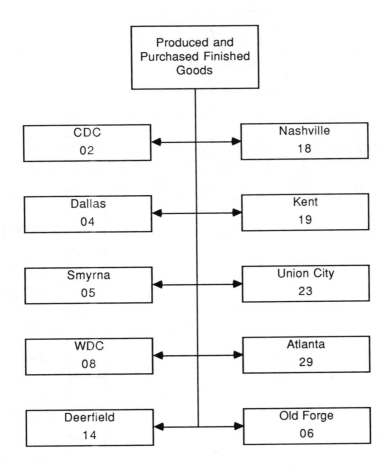

A MANUFACTURER OF CABINETS (CONT.)

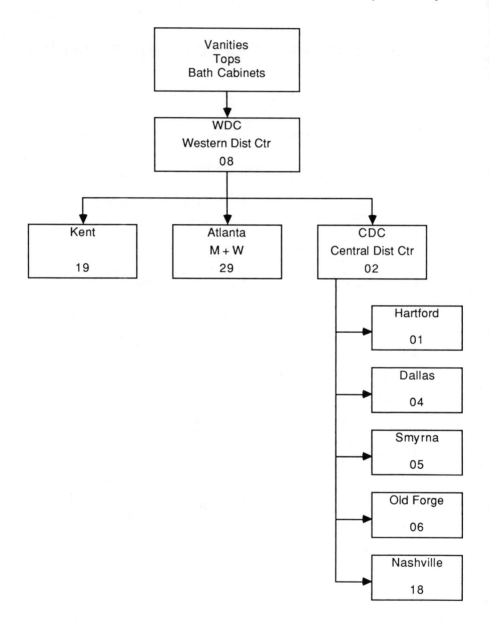

A MANUFACTURER OF MATTRESSES

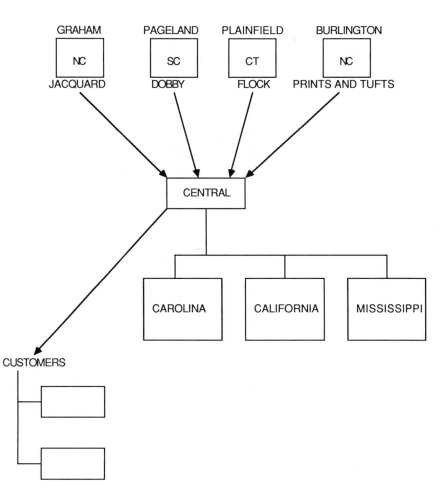

A MANUFACTURER OF MICROCOMPUTERS

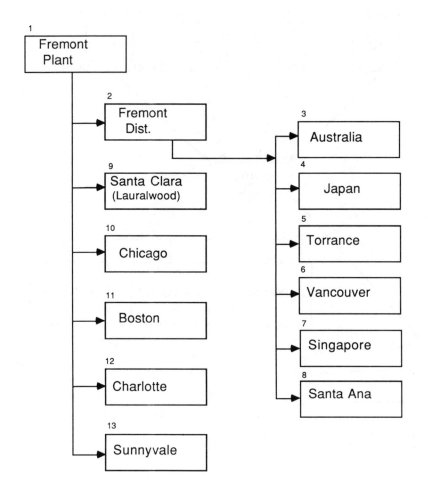

216

A STEEL PROCESSOR

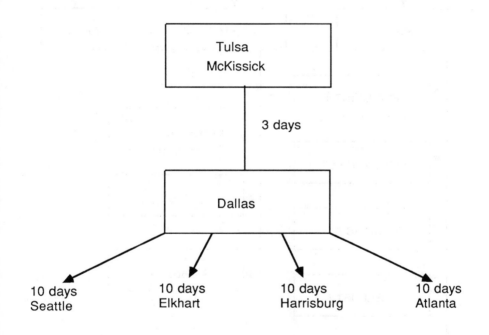

A WHOLESALER OF HEAVY HARDWARE

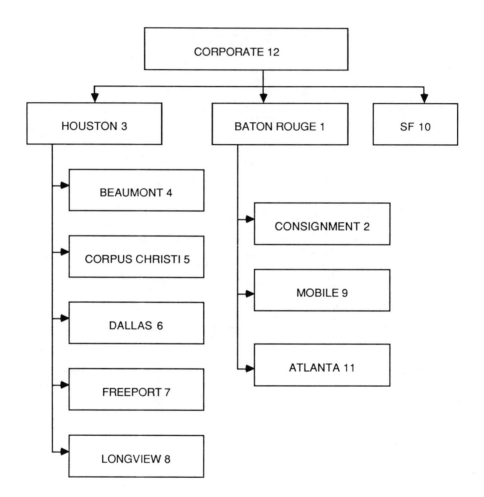

AN AUSTRALIAN MANUFACTURER

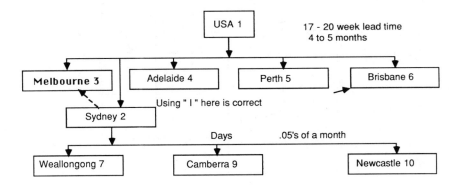

AN AUTOMOTIVE PART IMPORTER

BRANCH WORK

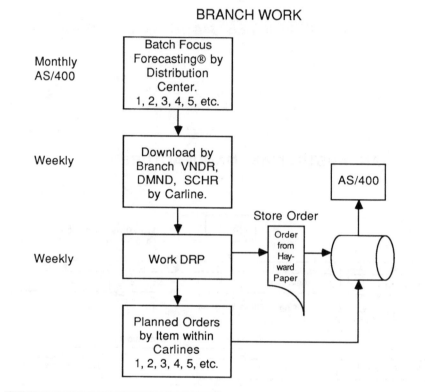

Monthly
AS/400

Batch Focus Forecasting® by Distribution Center. 1, 2, 3, 4, 5, etc.

Weekly

Download by Branch VNDR, DMND, SCHR by Carline.

AS/400

Weekly

Work DRP

Store Order

Order from Hayward Paper

Planned Orders by Item within Carlines 1, 2, 3, 4, 5, etc.

HAYWARD PURCHASING

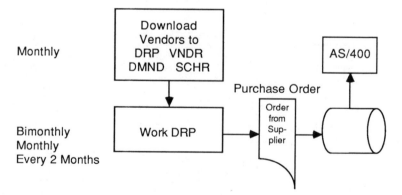

Monthly

Download Vendors to DRP VNDR DMND SCHR

AS/400

Bimonthly
Monthly
Every 2 Months

Work DRP

Purchase Order

Order from Supplier

AN EXPLOSIVES MANUFACTURER

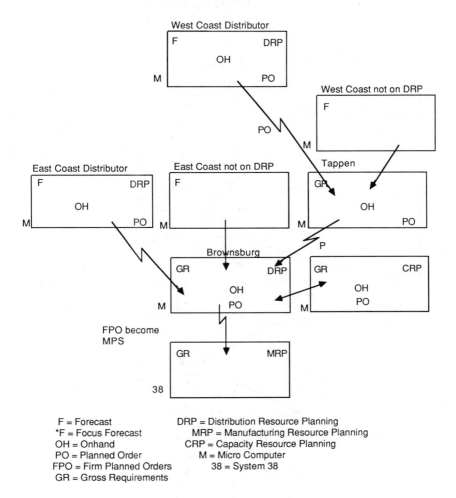

F = Forecast
*F = Focus Forecast
OH = Onhand
PO = Planned Order
FPO = Firm Planned Orders
GR = Gross Requirements

DRP = Distribution Resource Planning
MRP = Manufacturing Resource Planning
CRP = Capacity Resource Planning
M = Micro Computer
38 = System 38

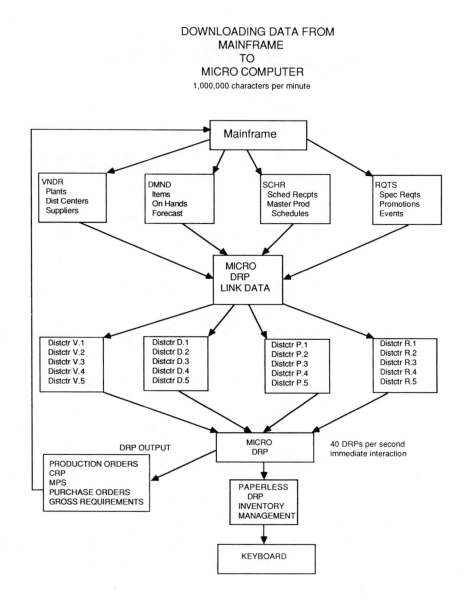

DOWNLOADING DATA FROM
MAINFRAME
TO
MICRO COMPUTER
1,000,000 characters per minute

Mainframe

VNDR
Plants
Dist Centers
Suppliers

DMND
Items
On Hands
Forecast

SCHR
Sched Recpts
Master Prod
Schedules

RQTS
Spec Reqts
Promotions
Events

MICRO
DRP
LINK DATA

Distctr V.1
Distctr V.2
Distctr V.3
Distctr V.4
Distctr V.5

Distctr D.1
Distctr D.2
Distctr D.3
Distctr D.4
Distctr D.5

Distctr P.1
Distctr P.2
Distctr P.3
Distctr P.4
Distctr P.5

Distctr R.1
Distctr R.2
Distctr R.3
Distctr R.4
Distctr R.5

DRP OUTPUT

MICRO
DRP

40 DRPs per second
immediate interaction

PRODUCTION ORDERS
CRP
MPS
PURCHASE ORDERS
GROSS REQUIREMENTS

PAPERLESS
DRP
INVENTORY
MANAGEMENT

KEYBOARD

A MANUFACTURER OF CHEMICALS

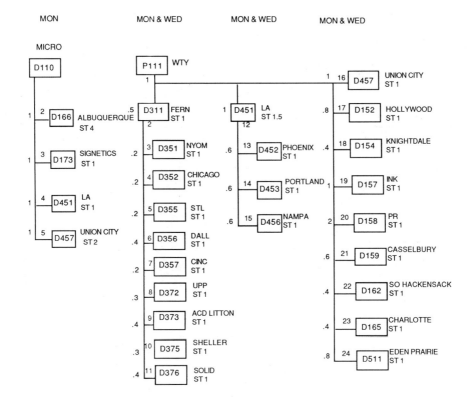

MON   MON & WED   MON & WED   MON & WED

MICRO

D110

P111 WTY

                                                              1 16 D457 UNION CITY
                                                                              ST 1

1 2 D166 ALBUQUERQUE   .5 D311 FERN   1 D451 LA   .8 17 D152 HOLLYWOOD
                    ST 4   ST 1   ST 1.5   ST 1

1 3 D173 SIGNETICS   .2 3 D351 NYOM   .6 13 D452 PHOENIX   .4 18 D154 KNIGHTDALE
                    ST 1   ST 1   ST 1   ST 1

1 4 D451 LA   .2 4 D352 CHICAGO   14 D453 PORTLAND 1 19 D157 INK
                    ST 1   ST 1   .6   ST 1   ST 1

1 5 D457 UNION CITY   .2 5 D355 STL   .6 15 D456 NAMPA   2 20 D158 PR
                    ST 2   ST 1   ST 1   ST 1

                          .4 6 D356 DALL   .6 21 D159 CASSELBURY
                                  ST 1   ST 1

                          .2 7 D357 CINC   .4 22 D162 SO HACKENSACK
                                  ST 1   ST 1

                          .3 8 D372 UPP   .4 23 D165 CHARLOTTE
                                  ST 1   ST 1

                          .4 9 D373 ACD LITTON   .8 24 D511 EDEN PRAIRIE
                                  ST 1   ST 1

                          .3 10 D375 SHELLER
                                   ST 1

                          .4 11 D376 SOLID
                                   ST 1

LEFT - Lead Time = weeks   RIGHT - Safety Time = weeks
            in transit   f/c error & delivery failure

223

Index